The
Land and People
❖ ❖ *of* IRAQ ❖ ❖

PORTRAITS OF THE NATIONS SERIES

The
Land *and* People
of IRAQ

BAHIJA LOVEJOY

Portraits of the Nations Series

J. B. LIPPINCOTT COMPANY
PHILADELPHIA · NEW YORK

The author wishes to thank the following for permission to use photographs:
The Metropolitan Museum of Art: pages 9 and 39.
Embassy of the Republic of Iraq: pages 13, 57, 109, 111, 142 and 146.
Arab Information Center: pages 17, 79, 104, 123 and 149.
University Museum, University of Pennsylvania: pages 43, 44 and 45.
Iraq Museum: page 58.
The Ministry of Guidance, Baghdad: page 113.

Contents

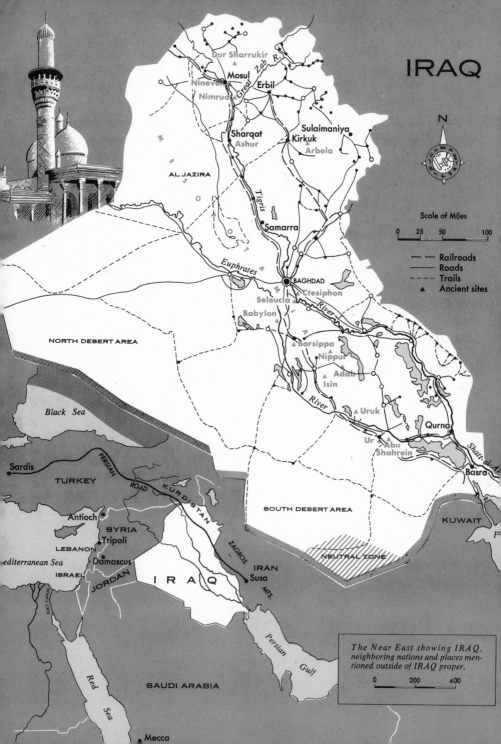

IRAQ

Dur Sharrukin ▲
Mosul
Nineveh
Nimrud ▲   Erbil
Great Zab R.

Sharqat
Ashur ▲   Kirkuk   Sulaimaniya
Arbela ▲

AL JAZIRA

M
E
S
O
P
O
T
A
M
I
A

Tigris

Samarra

Euphrates

BAGHDAD
Ctesiphon
Seleucia
Babylon ▲
River

NORTH DESERT AREA

Borsippa ▲
Nippur ▲
Adab ▲
Isin ▲

River

Uruk ▲

Ur ▲ Abu
Shahrein ▲

Qurna

Basra

Shatt-al-Arab

N

Scale of Miles

0   25   50   100

— — Railroads
——— Roads
- - - Trails
▲   Ancient sites

Black Sea

Sardis

TURKEY

PERSIAN

ROAD

KURDISTAN

ZAGROS MTS.

SOUTH DESERT AREA

KUWAIT

NEUTRAL ZONE

Antioch

SYRIA
Tripoli

LEBANON

Damascus

ISRAEL

JORDAN

I R A Q

IRAN
Susa

Mediterranean Sea

SUEZ CANAL

SAUDI ARABIA

Red Sea

Persian Gulf

Mecca

*The Near East showing IRAQ,
neighboring nations and places mentioned outside of IRAQ proper.*

0   200   400

❖ 1 ❖

The Land Between the Rivers

In the Middle East, south of the Turkish peninsula linking Asia to Europe, lies the modern republic of Iraq. It is a country of rich variety and contrast—of vast, arid deserts fringed by snow-capped mountains, of fertile plains stretching down to river valleys.

Here, it is believed, is one of the oldest regions in the world continuously inhabited by man. Because its earliest settlement has been dated at 6,000 years before Christ, it is called by many people "the cradle of civilization."

Memorable accounts have come down to us through the ages about this part of the world. Here were the Hanging Gardens of Babylon, one of the seven wonders of the ancient world. Many of the events described in the Bible took place on its sun-baked soil. Here was the site of the Garden of Eden. Here, too, was the setting for the fabulous tales of the Thousand and One Nights, and here was the birthplace of Sinbad the Sailor.

This country, in spite of its history dating back to antiquity, is very much a part of our modern world. For underneath its earth are millions and millions of gallons of oil, which are being pumped through pipelines to ships that carry it around the globe. The last time you rode in a car or a bus, its motor may have been powered with gasoline made from Iraq's oil. The country has justly been described as a desert floating upon a sea of oil.

Iraq is roughly triangular in shape. It is bordered by Turkey on the north; Iran on the east; the Persian Gulf (the country's sole outlet to the sea), Kuwait, and Saudi Arabia on the south; and Jordan and Syria on the west. It is about 530 miles from the apex of this triangle to the southernmost boundary, and roughly 495 miles from the most eastern border to the west. Altogether the country encompasses an area of approximately 171,000 square miles—this is slightly larger than the state of California—and has a population of barely seven million. The three largest cities are Mosul to the north, Baghdad, the capital, in the center, and Basra to the south.

Two giant rivers flow south from Turkey, down through Syria and northern Iraq to the rich delta land where they join to empty into the Persian Gulf. It is these rivers, the Tigris and the Euphrates, that have given the region its ancient name of Mesopotamia, from the Greek words meaning "land between the rivers." Since antiquity men have referred to this part of the world as the Fertile Crescent. The Bible mentions Mesopotamia, using the Aramaic words *Padan Aram,* meaning the "field of Aram." Aramaic was the language spoken by Jesus. Iraq, the country's modern name, from the Arabian word that means "a cliff," was given it by the Moslem followers of Mohammed when they occupied it in the seventh century A.D.

Iraq is an ancient land that saw the earliest beginning of recorded history and the first monumental architecture. There the first copper vessels were used, as well as the first wheel, plow, and battering ram, the first pictographic writing, mathematics, and astrology. Here were the first written laws, the first democratic type of government. In this region a highly developed civilization flourished at a time when the Egyptian pharaohs were only beginning to erect their colossal pyramids and when the continent of Europe was but a wilderness inhabited by barbaric nomads. Many and differing cultures existed here several thousands of years before Christianity. And so Mesopotamia, although far away on the other side of the continent of Europe, was of vital importance in the development of the West's cultural heritage.

Some of the earliest-known scenes in the drama of man were played in this region against a backdrop so vast that it saw the passing of many empires, races, and cultures. Between the days of the Sumerians, during the third millennium B.C., and World War I, when Iraq was placed under British mandate, many civilizations rose and fell. In peace and in war people came from across the desert and through the mountain passes to settle on the verdant shores of the rivers or in the plains at the mountains' base. Sumerians, Babylonians, Assyrians, Chaldeans, Persians, Greeks, Romans, Arabs, Mongols, Ottomans, and British all played their parts upon this stage. Some contributed enormously and bestowed great gifts. Others left havoc and devastation. And down through the years, like the desert sands since time immemorial, boundaries shifted and changed.

Alabaster winged bull, IX Century B.C. (885–860), a guardian of the Palace of Ashur-nasir-apal II at Kalhu, modern Nimrud.

The spade of the archaelogist is still uncovering fresh clues, and every year the frontier of our knowledge of man's beginning is pushed back a little more. It is now thought, for example, that Mesopotamia was the homeland of Abraham, who became the father of the Hebrew people. He lived for a long time, roughly from 1650 to 1550 B.C. Biblical events and figures are hard to fix into any specific place or time, but we know that it was about a thousand years later that the Jews walked in humiliation from Jerusalem to captivity in Nebuchadnezzar's Babylon. Alexander the Great lived only two hundred years after this. In his attempt (which was really quite successful) to unify the world as it existed then, he considered Mesopotamia a crossroads, and used it as a bridge to link the East and the West.

Here were fought titanic battles in the struggle between the two great empires of Persia and Rome—the former waxing in power, the latter on the wane—as both determined to control the routes leading from Europe to the fabulously rich eastern lands of India and the Orient. And in the eighth and ninth centuries A.D., during the height of the Islamic culture, the caliph Harun al-Rashid made Baghdad the center of world culture and power, the focus of wealth, learning, and art.

Peoples came and went, empires rose and fell, but this land has endured. If we pay a visit to Iraq today, we never completely lose the sense of being linked with the past. Spring is the most beautiful time of the year in this country. During this season a city schoolteacher is permitted to take her pupils to the country for a *safra,* or picnic. It is a tremendous treat for these children to be free of school-day regimentation, to go to play in the green countryside, for in the towns and cities of Iraq there are few parks as we know them, few shaded lawns or trees to sit beneath.

Let us go with them as they travel by car, bus, or train—or on foot if transportation is not available. As we stroll along with the children, we catch sight of strange-looking mounds that dot the landscape throughout the country. These mounds, or tells, are storehouses of antiquity. Within those as yet undisturbed by the archaeologist lie secrets of history hidden for perhaps thousands of years.

These great heaps of rubble have been covered by sandstorms that twisted and swirled through the ages. Under the dust, earth, and stones that have accumulated may lie a king's palace, a royal throne, some great piece of statuary, a golden harp, a warrior's chariot, or a queen's jewels of gold, precious stones, and lapis lazuli. Ancient mounds are, of course, not found only in Iraq, but no others anywhere else in the world go back so far. Level by level, some of the tells of Mesopotamia take us back through history and deep into prehistoric times.

Perhaps the children do not guess at what may be inside. But they can see that the freshets of spring have turned these mounds and the fields surrounding them into vast carpets of green, tapestried with wild flowers of a hundred colors: there are iris, poppies, anemones, tulips, sweet peas, clover, jasmine, camomile, and many more. The children like to pick them in great sweet-smelling bunches to take back to their homes in the town, unaware that some of these flowers now growing by the million are descended from plants which bloomed long ago in the garden of a caliph or the royal park of a king. These mounds are frequently found quite near a river or a bed where a river once was, for both great rivers have changed their courses over the years.

Let us take a look at the geography of the country as a whole. The climate and physical characteristics of Iraq deeply affect the way of life and working conditions of the people. The country is divided into four distinct sections: desert, mountains, central plains, and the southern alluvial delta. The steppe-and-desert region, a part of the Syrian and Arabian desert also, is known as *al Badiya* in Arabic. The flatland—broken here and there by uplands and rocky hills—is dry (almost rainless), sandy, and without trees. Across the steppes the nomadic Bedouin people wander in search of pasture for their flocks. In the winter and spring they are able to find some areas of sparse grass in the wadis, or hollows, that floodwaters have carved out of the rock through ages of erosive action. But most of the water sources are dry much of the year, and the Bedouin who live in the desert areas must move their flocks and camels in continuous migration, always looking for water and grass.

In contrast, the Kurdistan mountains to the northeast, separating Iraq from Iran, tower as high as 11,000 feet in some peaks, and are snow-capped several months of the year. Scattered villages cling to the mountain shelves; the houses are built of stone hewn from nearby ledges. There are no forests in Iraq. Here in the north there are just some thinly wooded sections of scrub oak, walnut, poplar, and pine. Even though it doesn't sound as though its soil could be very productive, this mountainous area is fine for vineyards and the growing of tobacco, in addition to summer grasses for sheep and goats.

In these northern mountains of Iraq are some of the most beautiful views in the Middle East. Here you can see majestic gorges, great valleys, waterfalls, and clear mountain springs that are a match for any in the world. It is a part of the country that is rapidly becoming a favorite vacation area for the Iraqi people and others. This upland region extends north of Baghdad, far beyond Mosul up to the Anti-Taurus range of mountains in southeastern Turkey.

The northern area between the two rivers (but south, of course, of the mountains) is called in Arabic *al Jazira,* which means "the island." This land is mostly a gently rolling plain that rises as high as 1,000 feet above sea level. In general it is fertile and productive, and in several regions there is sufficient rain for the growing of winter cereals, fruits, and vegetables.

The southern plains are very flat, and there is no stone to be found. But, although impregnated with salt, they are potentially fertile. The plains, about 100 miles in width, extend for a distance of 300 miles or more northward from the Persian Gulf. This is the delta land of the two rivers, and two thirds of present-day Iraq's arable land is located here.

The climate of Iraq is excessively hot in the summer and fairly mild in the winter. The spring is the loveliest season of all, but it, like the autumn, is very short indeed. Summer begins in May and continues into October, with normal midday temperature running as high as 115°. If you were to visit Baghdad in the height of the summer you would really feel as if you were in an oven. But the nights bring

A shepherd with his flock.

a little relief for, as in most desert regions, they are relatively cool. Winter lasts from November to April, and it is the season of rain. At this time of year the temperature can drop below 40°, but 45° is average.

The greatest amount of rainfall, because of the nearby mountains, is in the northern region of Mosul. Here the yearly average is 15 inches. In Baghdad, the central part of the country, it drops to 6 inches. The desert region has only a few inches of rainfall in all. There is only a little to the southeast, and the extensive agricultural program that is in practice here depends wholly upon irrigation. This is carried out by pumping water from rivers and canals. The network of irrigation canals in Iraq today is probably not nearly as extensive as it was in ancient Mesopotamia. Some of the ancient trenches uncovered recently have actually been put back into use. Today we are inclined to believe that the more modern something is, the better and more efficient it is likely to be. But in Iraq these Sumerian irrigation ditches of the third millennium B.C. have in some places proved as workable as those designed and constructed by today's engineers.

It is believed that the great flood described in the Bible took place in Mesopotamia, and that when Noah's Ark finally came to rest, it was on the 16,000-foot-high peak of Mount Ararat in the neighboring present-day country of Turkey. It is not far from there that the two rivers of Iraq, the Tigris and the Euphrates, have their sources. The Tigris twists and winds like a snake down its 1,130-mile length, and it is joined by several tributaries. One of the largest is the great Zab. Another is the Lesser Zab.

The Euphrates is about 1,480 miles long and flows through Turkey and Syria before entering Iraq. Its one tributary is in Syria. The Tigris is narrower, swifter, and carries more water than the Euphrates.

Silt deposits brought down by the two rivers over thousands of years of flooding and receding have reshaped the contour of the land, and in some places the river beds are actually above the level of the adjacent ground. In the spring, melting snow in the mountains of neighboring Turkey, where both rivers have their sources, cause floods that are often disastrous. But today, thanks to income from oil, the government is able to spend millions on a vast irrigation, drainage, and flood-control program. When this program is in full operation, it will eliminate most of the danger of annual floods and also supply, from huge man-made lakes, an abundance of water the year around. Through these methods it will be possible to reclaim thousands of acres of what is now useless and arid land.

The Tigris and Euphrates join at Qurna, and the river that then flows down into the Persian Gulf is called the Shatt-al-Arab, "the river of the Arabs." If we look at an ancient map of this region, however, we might not see it marked at all, for centuries ago the Shatt-al-Arab probably did not exist and the two rivers, therefore, entered the gulf by separate mouths. Even the shore of the gulf itself would have looked different.

But the proud and majestic date palms look to us as though they had lined the two sides of the river forever. Since time immemorial they have constituted one of the chief sources of nourishment for a

Water wheels on the Euphrates.

large segment of the Iraqi people. Iraq produces eighty per cent of the world's date supply, and the finest. Dates are second only to oil in dollar volume of export.

If it is true, as Herodotus wrote, that "Egypt was the gift of the Nile," it might also be said that Iraq is the gift of the Tigris and Euphrates. A great deal of the nation's life revolves around these two rivers and their tributaries. As a matter of fact, Iraqi rarely refer to them separately, but speak of them as *al-Rafidayn,* a collective noun meaning "two rivers." The greater part of the population lives in the river basins. For centuries villages, towns, and cities were built as close as possible to the water—some right on the riverbank. This is true today in modern Iraq, and it is true particularly of the three cities of Baghdad, Basra, and Mosul.

Ruins of the great settlements of antiquity reveal that they too were situated on one of the great rivers. But over the years the courses of the rivers changed and turned away from these cities and their surroundings. And so once thriving communities were deserted and fell into ruin and oblivion. These lost cities, such as Babylon, have been brought to light again after thousands of years by nineteenth- and twentieth-century archaeologists.

The Shatt-al-Arab is one of Iraq's main highways. On its waters ply both old and new forms of transport. A steamboat, motorboat, or speedboat can be seen any day whizzing by the slower boats of ancient design—the *balam,* much like our canoe, or a raft that is buoyed up by inflated skins, or even the acorn-shaped *gufa,* now virtually extinct. As a matter of fact, these boats are not used only to get around on—hundreds of people live in them, especially in the marshlands of the south.

In many parts of southwest Asia one can see smoke and flame issuing out of the many oil and natural-gas seeps. Since the dawn of history gases from the oil deposits have burned incessantly, and by tradition it was into one of these "fiery furnaces" that Nebuchadnezzar thrust Shadrach, Meshach, and Abednego some 2,500 years ago. And it was from the asphalt, or bitumen, deposits in the vicinity of the Tigris and Euphrates that Noah, constructing his ark, sealed it "within and without with pitch"—another name for bitumen.

Iraqi fisherman on the Shaat-al-Arab.

Revenue from Iraq's oil fields runs into the hundreds of millions of dollars, and a large percentage of this is used by the government for human welfare, through a vast program of national development and construction. This program includes the much-needed flood control; rehabilitation of rural areas; public health and preventive medicine; hospital construction and road building; land reform, and the training of thousands for public service. It embraces also plans for the widening of educational facilities, from preschool through university and adult education levels. These ambitious plans, already implemented in urban areas, are now being put into effect in the rural or outlying districts.

Iraq today is as strategically centered as it was in ancient times when trade routes crossed the country from the Mediterranean lands to India and Asia Minor. Perhaps her neighbors in the Middle East are as well located, are as much of a bridge between the east and west, north and south. And all, including Iraq, are underdeveloped, their people poor. But none is so fortunate as Iraq, with her abundance of fertile land, her untapped resources, plenty of water, and with no overpopulation problems. Most important of all, there is the seemingly limitless sea of oil flowing under Iraq, Iran, Kuwait, Qatar, and Saudi Arabia, containing a fourth or more of the world's known supply of petroleum. The income from her share of this oil has given Iraq a good start on her program for the full development of her resources.

❖ 2 ❖

A Mosaic of Peoples and Religions

THE CONSTANT and continuous shifting of peoples from one area of Iraq to another, the waves of migration of many sorts of people from surrounding regions, and foreign occupation over the centuries have resulted, as you might expect, in a great mixture of peoples. This makes it hard to decide exactly to what race the Iraqi of today belong.

One fact is certain: most of the seven million who make up the population of the country are of the Arabian desert, and come from what we call Semitic stock. The word "Semitic" is actually better applied to language rather than race; it belongs among that ancient grouping that includes Assyrian, Aramaic, Syrian, Canaanite, Phoenician, Arabic, and Ethiopic.

But somehow Iraq did not become a "melting pot." The Kurds in the north remain Kurds, much as they have through the centuries, with their own well-defined language and culture. The nomadic Bedouin tribesmen of the desert are not like them at all, in looks or in the way they live and talk. And they in turn differ greatly from the southern marsh people who spend their time in boats on the delta lands close to the Persian Gulf. Of course in the cities and larger towns there are Iraqi who have been attracted by hopes of higher education, a steadier sort of job, and a richer life in general, and these have intermingled enough to form some sort of an urban composite. But the peoples in the mountains and deserts and plains have remained separate and distinct; the inevitable changes that take place as generation succeeds generation did not manage to weld them together into any kind of homogeneous whole.

Many things go to explain this, but two are the most important: the great diversity of the physical conditions, and the inadequacy, or complete lack, of communication between communities. These have restricted movement and commerce generally, isolated many communities completely, and hindered the natural growth and development of the population as a whole. To this day most of the roads are unsurfaced, impassable for a large part of the year. Even if a road were there today, it might not be tomorrow, for a flash flood could wash it out overnight. Both the Tigris and Euphrates are used to some extent for transportation, but they are only navigable downstream. This is particularly true in the upper reaches. While the rivers are wider in the south, they are shallow, and only flat-bottomed boats can ply up and down them. Most Iraqi find the railroad fare much too high for their means, and use the train only when it is absolutely necessary.

These are the factors that divide the country into such very separate parts—or, it might be more accurate to say, that maintain the divisions put into effect centuries ago. It is a land of diversity, inhabited by a mosaic of peoples who differ in cultural traditions, social customs, dress, diet, and ways of life. And it is these differences that set Iraq apart from any other Middle Eastern country.

Suppose we visit a fairly good-sized town toward the center of the country and take a look at the mixture of people we find there. If we walk into the souk, or market place, we will probably think it too crowded, smelly, and noisy for comfort; but we will find it an exciting place also, buzzing with activity and clamorous with the babel of many different tongues. It is made vivid for us by the strange costumes of the Bedouin tribesmen, the farmers from the plains, and the marsh Arabs from the south. Here and there we can pick out an Iraqi who is fair of skin, with yellow hair and piercing blue eyes. But for the most part the people we see bartering their goods are swarthy and short, with dark hair and eyes. At first glance their clothing is very much the same. Most of the men wear a long, loose-fitting white shirt. It is covered by a big, black or brown shawl, or aba. Nearly all wear a headdress made up of a rather large kerchief, a *kuffiyeh,* that stretches from the forehead to below the neck at the back, and this is held in place by an *agal.* Many are barefoot; others wear clogs or loose-fitting slippers.

If we are accompanied by a guide, he can tell us what to look for and how to distinguish among the natives, and we will see that the mountain Kurds are not only dark and weather-beaten, but also a bit terrifying in their unusual tunics, belted by many guns and knives. Our guide can certainly point out the Chaldeans who live in the northern villages around Mosul, because they have on baggy white trousers under their cloaks and wear gay, brightly embroidered vests; he also shows us the fierce-looking Assyrians.

If there are some of the Yezidi tribe in the souk, our eye is caught by the women's unusual headdresses, looped with gold coins, and by their necklaces of amber, colored stones, or glass, depending on their wealth. Yezidi men wear a characteristic, round-necked shirt that is usually white. This is a strange tribe indeed, for its members are devil appeasers. They believe in one God, but they nevertheless try to appease *shaytan,* or Satan, because they think that the forces of evil are stronger and more active in the world than are the forces of good.

Turning away, we might be surprised to catch sight of a girl, walking across the square, wearing a suit or gown copied straight from Paris. It might very easily happen, and she makes quite a contrast to the Moslem woman who is sitting by the side of the road, selling a bowl of yogurt or eggs: she is dressed from head to foot in black, and her face is veiled. There would be several men in European dress in the souk, but they might have a tarboosh (fez), or a little hat like a sailor's that is called a *sidarah,* on their heads.

All these people mingle in the teeming, seething marketplace, buy-

Yezidis at Sheik'Adi.

ing what they need and selling their wares before returning to their homes. The noisiness that we are a part of becomes hard to take in the afternoon sun. It is difficult to reconcile the cheerful bustle we see at the market with the harsh frugality of the lives of most of the people there.

In order to see what these Iraqi are like and to understand their ways, we will have to visit several of them in the places where they live and work, eat, and take their rest. Perhaps we will even be able to enjoy their hospitality—politeness and generosity to a guest are profoundly held traditions in this Moslem land.

Since our market town is pretty much in the center of Iraq, let us start with a trip to an agricultural settlement not far from where we are, on the alluvial plain between the two rivers. It is here that the typical Iraqi live—the fellahin, or farmers, who make up two thirds of the population and are the basis of the country's economy. The working conditions of the fellahin in this particular village are very much like those in the many other farming settlements scattered all through the northeastern, central, and lower parts of the river valley. But the way of life, the dialect or language itself, the diet and clothes can vary a great deal from one community to another, even though the distance separating them is only a few miles. Such startling differences in custom are particularly true in the Mosul district to the north.

In the village we have chosen, we have been invited to visit the house of a man named Ali. As we follow him and enter the house, we see nothing at first. Few village huts have windows, and no windows have glass or anything to protect you from the weather or let in the light. There are, of course, practically no electricity, running water, or plumbing facilities in these rural areas, but plants for nationwide electrification are well beyond the planning stage.

Ali is dressed in typical fashion in the *thawb* (a loose shirt), belt, and a headdress of black cloth. His wife squats beside a basin of laundry near by. She is wearing a loose, gaily colored gown, with black kerchief gray from the dust. Ali introduces us, and points to the *geel* she is using instead of soap. *Geel,* he tells us, is a kind of greasy mud that is dug out of the hillside especially for this purpose. We sit down on mats of straw or pressed wool that lie on the dirt floor. As our eyes become used to the dim light, we can make out the interior of the hut, which Ali tells us is much like the others in the village. He explains that the reason they were built so close together was for protection against marauding Bedouin tribesmen; but he goes on to tell us with some pride that the government is pretty successful in putting a stop to their raids these days.

We see that the house is built of a cement made of straw and mud, with wooden roof beams. Ali tells us that farther north the fellahin may find stone out of which to build their houses. Everything looks

Iraqi farmer.

drab. There is no furniture, only a plain wooden chest for storage. The red-woolen comforter rolled up on top of it provides the room's only note of color. Ali shows us the courtyard at the back, where he keeps his donkey and his goat.

He used to be employed, he tells us, by a *mallak,* or absentee landlord, who rented all the land on which the village lies from the government and leased it out to agricultural laborers. In the old days he was allowed to keep for himself half of the wheat and vegetables he grew for his mallak. Until very recently, only a few fellahin actually owned their own land, and most of these lived farther north. Some, like Ali, split their yield fifty-fifty with the landlord. Others got even less. An overseer collected what was due. The *fellah* naturally felt little attachment to his landlord, and in many cases never set eyes on him. Today, however, Ali and other farmers like him are working on land they own. It was distributed by the government through the Agrarian Reform Policy. Ali uses more modern methods, too, including machinery, and will benefit from irrigation projects which are under way.

Ali's ties are basically to his family, to the land, the village, his religion, and to the tribe to which his family belonged before it settled down. We get up from the floor of the hut and follow him outside for a tour of the village. Here, too, there is a market place with a blacksmith's forge and a grocery shop. We enter and find it is the Arab version of our own country store; it contains everything from food and tobacco to bolts of cloth and exotic, sweet-smelling herbs used for medicinal purposes. We stroll past the coffeehouse, filled now with gesticulating Arabs, who sit after their day's work and sip the thick Turkish brew as they listen to the one radio in the village. It blares out a mixture of news bulletins, political oratory, Arabian music, or American jazz tunes played in a strange tempo. Behind the store, and visited continually by a string of men and women, is a small shrine to Allah. Ali tells us that in the next village there is a good-sized mosque. Ninety-four per cent of all Iraqi are Moslem. There are other religions besides that of Islam: about three per cent are Christian, mostly to be found around Mosul to the north. There are about 10,000 Jews in Baghdad (most of the 150,000 listed in the 1947 census have since moved to Israel). There are, in addition to the devil-worshiping Yezidis we mentioned before, the Mandaeans or Sabaeans, who base their faith on the rites of baptism and are sometimes called the Christians of St. John. They live in the river country to the south.

Ali is proud of the fact that his village, though it is small, does have a school where his five children go to learn to read and write. They speak Arabic, but a little English is also taught. We ask him what he and his family eat, and he answers that bread, from the wheat he grows, is their staple food together with dates. He gets milk from his goat to make yogurt and cheese, he drinks tea and coffee, and sometimes has tomatoes, onions, or a little fruit if the crop has been good.

From our conversation with Ali and our visit to his rural home, we can see that the life of the Iraqi farmer is full of hardship. He and his whole family toil the year round, in fair weather or poor, watching the sky for rain and praying to Allah (God) for a good yield. For crop failure, whether it is caused by an overly severe storm, by hail, flood, drought, or clouds of locusts, can mean starvation and utter disaster for them all. But the weather is not the only thing that makes life difficult for Ali. Everything is antiquated—the work methods, the tools, even the way of life, which has changed so little over the centuries. Ali's ancestors, living perhaps before the Bible was written, used very much the same sort of plow, drawn by the same type of animal and maybe even over the same plot of land.

Up until now the fellahin have had few goals, and little incentive for improvement. But today the government is taking steps to make life easier for them generally. It is a long, slow process. Ali and those like him rarely complain however. Conditioned by years of hardship, they believe that whatever happiness or misfortune comes their way, it is Kismet, or the will of Allah—written forever on the tablets of the Koran, without possibility of change.

Taking leave of Ali, we journey southward. We go through Qurna and beyond Basra to where the Tigris and Euphrates join to become Shatt-al-Arab. At the site of the legendary Garden of Eden we meet Nasir Salim, a marsh Arab who is going to take us in his *balam* down through the lagoons and swamps till we reach his village, less than fifty miles from the Persian Gulf. Before starting out, Nasir shows us an ancient thorn tree and says with a shrug and a smile that this is the original Tree of Knowledge, but we see no apples on it. Nasir knows the kind of information that will interest tourists.

He is a tall man, strong-looking, with a fine black beard. He wears a kuffiyeh. His is gayer than the usual Arab headgear, for it is white with bright-red checks and border and makes a striking contrast to his black cloak. His loose-fitting white shirt is hitched up in his belt, so that his legs are bare. We understand the reason for this when he motions to us to sit down in his flat-bottomed, pitch-sealed boat, because he takes up a towing line and for the first part of our trip marches along the flat, boggy grass by the side of the river, pulling us behind him.

We are now in the vast 6,000 square miles of swamp and marsh land that surround the lower sections of the two rivers and Shatt-al-Arab. It looks very different down here from the view that every traveler flying to India, the Far East, or some port of the Persian Gulf has had pointed out to him from the air. Not many foreigners have actually penetrated these murky lagoons, which are very much like the bayous down around New Orleans. Here live an odd and primitive people known as the Ma'dan, a word that connotes "black country." The plains farmers and even the Bedouin fear them be-

Marsh Arabs.

cause of their strangeness and inaccessibility. Those of a less diverse background look down on them also because of their lineage—a mixture of Arabian, Sumerian, Babylonian, and Persian.

We slip past whole communities perched precariously beside the waterways that crisscross each other interminably. It is plain that the waterway is the focal point of the marsh Arab's entire way of life; it is his street, and the *balam* is the only mode of transportation available to him as he goes from one island village to another in search of a buyer for his produce. Nasir tells us that his son Hadji could handle this canoelike boat before he could walk.

In addition to the water that we see everywhere, we are most struck by the giant reeds, some 20 feet high or more, that grow all around. We ask Nasir about them, and he says that his people use them for just about everything. As we approach the cluster of straw-built huts that make up his village, he explains that there is no stone, wood, or even brick to use for building materials. And so they use the reeds. They tie them together in bundles much like a haycock, and pile them one on top of another for the frame of the house. Flat mats are fastened to this frame to seal the walls and roof. In summertime the house is cool and pleasant, for it is open at both ends; unlike the hut of the fellahin, it is light and airy as the breeze off the water blows in and out. The one thing that seems peculiar to us as we enter Nasir's house is the platform of reeds that has been built in its center at about eye level. We learn that he, his wife and children squat up there in time of flood—and the floods are inevitable in this part of the country.

Outside again, we look around the village. Little children are running about naked, and the women are unveiled. Some of the houses seem larger and far more elaborate than others, and Nasir explains that these are used as guest houses for the sheik. They tower above us, with great arches and ribbed vaults that look very much like the reproductions of ancient Sumerian temples in the museums (the boats of those earlier days also look exactly the same as the one we were in). Like the people of the marshlands today, the Sumerians of 5,000 years ago made good use of the giant reeds, not only for purposes of building, but also as a supplement to their diet. Today the animals are given its young shoots as fodder.

Down in the south the water buffalo is of vital importance in the life of the Ma'dan. These animals are raised for sale. They sometimes work as beasts of burden, pulling the laden *balam* from the riverbank, and they provide the Arab family with milk, cream, buttermilk, and cheese. Their dung is used for fuel.

Because there are no trees except the palms from which to get sticks and planks, the Ma'dan have adapted the plentiful reeds to many and varied uses. They are clever at fashioning beds, cribs, chairs and other furniture, as well as in making baskets, trays, and chicken coops. Some of the people excel in such handicraft, and make quilts, colored rugs, and mats that are not only used in their own community but are also sold to merchants in the nearest towns.

You would probably find life far more interesting in this part of Iraq than in the agricultural community where our fellah friend lived and worked. It is certainly very different from any preconceived notion we might have had of how the Arab people live. You would enjoy some of the activities very much, such as the spear fishing in the marshes, or the catching of waterfowl among the reeds. Because of the things he can catch, the Ma'dan is able to enrich somewhat the diet of dairy products and the rice naturally grown in such a watery countryside. But like nearly all the rural poor Iraqi, the Ma'dan do not eat meat, unless an animal is sick and has to be killed or unless they have a guest. One or two of them may own a cow, and perhaps a few chickens.

Nasir Salim and his people are considered the most backward in the country. They are in general ignorant and illiterate. If illness strikes, they are usually too poor to go to an urban clinic or fetch a doctor to such an outlying region. But, as Nasir has proved, they are like most of their countrymen—generous, friendly, and hospitable once a stranger has been accepted in their midst.

Turning northward, away from the marshy terrain of the Ma'dan, we continue beyond Baghdad to the west and come to al Jazira— that desert land lying between the Tigris and Euphrates rivers as they branch toward Syria and Turkey like the arms of a giant *V*. Following a track across the plain, we look into the far distance at a cluster of strange, square-topped tents, etched black against the horizon. It is there that we are about to meet Ahmad Hassam, the son of a Bedouin chief, who will tell us about the nomadic tribesmen of the desert that are his people.

We pass a herd of gazelles, those most beautiful of all desert animals, glorified throughout Arab literature by poets who often compare their grace, length of neck, and shape of eye to the charms of the women they love. On the right, close to the settlement that is our destination, a group of women are dismantling tents and loading their belongings onto the backs of camels. On close inspection we see that the tents actually are black in color, and are made from goat or camel hair. As we stand there staring, we are approached by Ahmad, our guide and host. He appears a romantic figure as he sits erect on his wiry desert pony, his cape billowing out behind him, his gaunt, weather-seamed face framed in a white kerchief. But we learn from him that there is nothing romantic about life in the desert. On the contrary, he tells us, it is very hard and uncertain, and he points to the women who are moving away now with the long camel caravan—they are searching for a new site.

As the son of a chief, Ahmad has had a certain amount of education in town, and he is able to explain to us the problems peculiar to his people. The Bedouin are constantly on the move, forced by necessity to seek pasturage for the animals on whom their existence depends. They even refer to themselves as the *Ruhal,* or Arabs "on the move." Exposed to the great heat of summer and bitter cold of winter, the nomads of the desert are in a constant battle with nature. They are very poor, Ahmad tells us, in part because the raiding of villages of other tribes, which in former days did much to bolster the fortunes of the Bedouin, has been stopped almost completely by the government. Camel-trading was once a source of income, but motor transport is reducing the need for camels, and the desert Arab is notoriously contemptuous of those who engage in agriculture or crafts to make a living. Subsistence therefore, though it doesn't take much, is difficult, and for some years now the government and certain of the wealthier sheiks, Ahmad's father among them, have been encouraging the Bedouin to settle on the land; its cultivation yields far more than the pasturage of animals. Many of these sheiks, incidentally, now own individually the land that once belonged to the tribe whose combined effort helped them to wealth and prestige. Ahmad's uncle, he tells us with pride, settled in the city many years ago, and is now a member of parliament. Another of his relatives has helped in the formation of a new political party to speak up for the Iraqi of the desert. Unfortunately progress is slow, because the average Bedouin looks down on the *hadar,* or tribesmen who have settled in the towns.

The Bedouin, numbering roughly 250,000, live in great poverty; in fact they are among the poorest and least educated of all ethnic groups in the country. For the most part they are occupied in the raising of sheep, camels, goats, donkeys, and horses and they have great influence on the economic life of Iraq, because of the export of these animals to other countries. Catching our glance at the thin, barefoot children playing near by, Ahmad tells us that while the birth rate among Bedouin is high, many children die in infancy, but those who survive grow up tough and wiry.

Sitting at the entrance to his tent and gazing out at the flat, dusty terrain in front of him, Ahmad describes the life of an average tribesman. His needs are few. He may spend a whole day in journeying to the nearest town or city with wool sheared from his sheep the day before. Perhaps it is hides he is selling, or a fat lamb he has slaughtered. He will barter it for coffee, sugar, flour, and rice. If he is able to get cash in the exchange, he might buy a saddle, a ring for his wife, or yardage to make clothing for his children. Perhaps he will buy a *thawb* or a belt for himself. As our host talks, we look around at the men and women working near us or walking by. They all go barefoot, and all are clad in the same kind of long shirt topped by a cloak.

The smell of coffee is strong, and Ahmad enters through the flap of his tent to bring us a cup of the thick brew that is the staple beverage. As we drink he tells of the Bedouin diet. It consists of bread, dates, and rice, and for drinking, besides coffee, there is leban or yogurt mixed with water, or camel's milk. Meat is a luxury, only eaten if an animal is too sick for further use. As we were told all over the country, if a guest comes, it is a different story, and almost always assures the roasting of a lamb, even if it is the only one the owner has. Everything will be shared with the guest, even if he is an enemy. Once he has dismounted and touched the rope of the tent, he is safe from harm and will be fed and sheltered. This is the tradition of the Iraqi. Like all his fellow believers, the desert Arab never complains, no matter how great his poverty and ignorance, and the harshness of his life. The name of Allah is continually on his lips. He holds that God is the fate to whom all must bow, and He is the cause of good and evil, of life and death.

Next to his devotion to God, the Bedouin owes allegiance to his family, his kin, and his *qabilah,* or tribe. Ahmad explains that the sheik, his father, is the leader of this particular settlement. He serves as a sort of governor and, assisted by other senior members, acts as a judge, performs marriages, and settles family disputes. It is he who collects the taxes for the government and makes the decisions as to what is best for the tribe as a whole. He is, in effect, responsible for its welfare. We ask Ahmad if he will succeed his father, and he tells us with simple sincerity that he will if he is good enough. The office is a hereditary one, but certain necessary qualifications must be fulfilled: courage, horsemanship, generosity, hospitality, and a sense of justice. It is possible to depose a sheik if he fails to measure up. We realize that this type of government has existed in the desert for hundreds and hundreds of years, and we see that the day-to-day existence of the nomads has changed little since the time of Abraham.

Leaving Ahmad and his Bedouin settlement, we strike north once more to Mosul and beyond on the final lap of our visit among the people of Iraq. In the mountains of southern Kurdistan that run from the Iranian border through the foothill regions, the Kurdish people live. The Iraqi Kurds are but one of the Kurdish tribes living in this sparsely populated region that borders on Turkey, the Soviet Union, and Iran. The Kurds of Iraq, numbering over a million, lead

Entrance to Tawela, a town in northern Iraq.

a vastly different life from other Iraqi, and live in an environment utterly unlike anything we have seen in the south. Plainly Indo-European or Aryan in origin, Kurdish tribes have existed in this part of the world since the dawn of history. These hardy mountain warriors, taller and more strongly built than the fellahin, are believed to be the Karduchi who forced the retreat of Xenophon's 10,000 soldiers in 401 B.C. The Sultan Saladin, who fought in the third Crusade in 1189, was a Kurd from these mountains.

The region of the Kurds was occupied by the Moslem Arabs in the seventh century A.D., in their victorious sweep through this part of the world, and the Kurds adopted Islam instead of Zoroaster as their religion. They were permitted to retain their own autonomy pretty much until the time of the Ottoman Turks, when their history became joined to that of the country of Iraq as a whole. Throughout the centuries, however, they never lost their identity or their own language, and they never gave up their dream of an independent Kurdistan.

At the end of World War I in the Treaty of Sèvres, dictated by the victorious powers to the defeated Ottoman Turks, there was a provision for the recognition of an independent Kurdistan. This was never ratified by Turkey, and the 1923 Treaty of Lausanne made no mention of a Kurdish state. It was at this point that the rebellion of the Kurds against the central Iraq government began, and it has continued to this day. The Kurdish rebellion, always simmering and frequently erupting into outright violence, found its strongest leaders among the Barzani family. Mulla Mustafa Barzani, the current head of the revolt, had been permitted to return to Baghdad after the 1958 revolution by Kassem, who promised to do all he could to help the Kurds. This peaceful state of affairs did not last long, however, and soon Mustafa was once again in the mountains, fighting and resisting the Iraqi forces attempting to quell the rebellion. He also made several attempts to bring the case of the Kurds up before the UN.

Some of the Kurds are wholly nomadic herdsmen, organized in tribes. They live in tents, camping on the plains during the winter months and pasturing high on the mountainside in summer. Resenting laws made outside their own region, they acknowledge no leadership but that of their own chief or headman. He is dependent on their good will for his power and authority, and he is appointed by the male members of the tribe. It is for the most part this nomadic element of the Kurds that causes trouble for the central government of Iraq, through their intransigence and dreams of a separate Kurdish state to be carved from parts of Turkey, Iraq, Iran, and the Soviet Union.

Many of these mountain people, however, have long ago settled in the villages and live as farmers. Their economy is based on agriculture combined with herding, and their methods are less primitive that those of the fellahin to the south. They raise wheat, barley, tobacco, cotton, rice, peas, and lentils. These Kurds are freeholders, farmers, sharecroppers, or laboring men, devoted to their farms and mountain pastures. Most believe in Islam and belong to the Sunni sect, but some Kurdish Christian sects cluster around Mosul. Those of the Kurds who are Yezidis, and believe in the appeasing of Satan, live for the most part in the Jebel mountain region near Mosul. Here, as elsewhere in the country, Arabic is the official language and is taught in the schools. However, Kurdish is also taught in this northern region.

To see the Kurdish people for ourselves, we journey east of Mosul to a village perched on a hillside above a rushing stream. Signs of the Kurdish rebellion are not very apparent here. The huts we walk past look more substantial than those in the south, because rock and stone are available for building purposes in this part of the country. Most of the houses are made of mud, or rock with mud as mortar, and huddle so close to one another that the flat roofs overlap. We meet Bakr, our Kurdish guide, who tells us that during the hot summer months these flat roofs are used for sleeping, and as a gathering place for family and friends. Bakr is dressed in the bright costume of the Kurds, with white shirt and baggy trousers thrust into scarlet leather boots with upturned points. Over his wide sash he wears a Zouave jacket embroidered in gold, and his skullcap is also embroidered and wrapped around with rolled-up kerchiefs. His dagger is curved, pointed, and richly ornamented. We see that the women here are also dressed very colorfully, with more freedom of movement than their black-caped sisters to the south. Bakr takes us inside his house, which he tells us is like most others in the village. In the center of the largest room is a hearth, and smoke from its fire wafts out through door and window. At the back is an enclosed yard for the donkey, cattle, and horses of the household. Its surrounding wall protects them from the icy wind that sweeps down from the Zagros Mountains looming high above the village.

We sit on the felt rug spread out on the floor, and Bakr brings us steaming tea from a samovar set on a brazier in the corner of the room. Pointing to the glasses set on a copper tray, our host tells us that Kurds drink tea many times a day, and the samovar is kept full. The tea is sweet and very strong, and with it we eat the sour, good, dark bread Bakr gives us. He says that it is the mainstay of his diet. Meat, however, is more frequently eaten here than in the south. There is plenty of water available for the mountain people, and this makes for better sanitary conditions. Nevertheless here, too, mortality is high.

We learn from Bakr that his people are poor, that there is much malaria among them, and that the severity of the weather makes their life hard. He has long been thinking, he tells us, of moving to the town of Sulaimaniya, at the foot of the mountain, which is the largest town of southern Kurdistan. He does not wish to be involved in the fighting to the north, and he believes he can profit more there from the government's development programs to improve living conditions, schools, and hospitals.

While many of the older inhabitants of Iraq live and die without ever having seen a community of any size, the young people, whether fellahin, Ma'dan, Kurds, or Bedouin, are beginning to filter into cities and towns. The nomad, for example, is making the trip to Mosul on the desert's edge to sell or barter his products, while his sheik goes to Baghdad, the capital and seat of the country's government, to represent his tribe or *liwa* in parliament. A wealthy and educated Kurd might move his family to the capital, so that he may engage in commerce or vie for some administrative post. A fellah, leaving his family behind in the village, might journey to Kirkuk in the north and work in the oil fields as an unskilled laborer or mechanic. Or he might work in the city in a coffee house, hotel or restaurant, or for one of the exclusive social clubs. A family from the Ma'dan might come north to the capital with water buffalo, sheep, and chickens. They will sell milk, eggs, and other products in the market or peddle from door to door, meanwhile building a *sarifa,* or hut of reeds and mud, on the outskirts or on a vacant lot adjacent to some modern housing project or villa. Another Ma'dan perhaps works in the date industry, opens a shall shop, or works as an apprentice in one of the craft shops in the souk.

But it is not easy to adjust to a new environment, and the great gap between city and country is a cleavage that exists in the very society of Iraq itself. In spite of the trend toward more urban living, the inhabitants of towns and cities still make up but one third of the country's population, and they are dependent on the rural villages for tax income, as well as for raw materials for industry and commerce. The trend continues, however, for the lures are great: a chance at regular employment, higher income and therefore a better living standard, better housing, and access to improved educational and health services.

Western influence is apparent socially and physically within the cities, where the old and new meet. The paved streets, wide avenues along which people walk in modern dress, the new hotels with up-to-date plumbing, and the neon signs all contrast markedly with covered bazaars and narrow, twisting side streets and alleys that take one back to the Arabian Nights. And at the city's edge are the mud huts and the way of life that have changed little in hundreds of years.

These are the people of Iraq, with their differing creeds and ethnic origins. All of them work, pray, do business together, and meet in the souk, the public baths, a country shrine or city mosque. When outside danger threatens, they will fight side by side, and they pray to the same God in time of drought or famine. But with such diverse ways of living, trouble is bound to erupt. Generally speaking, however, the amount of friction is small.

3

The Cradle of Ancient Empires

DISCOVERIES MADE by archaeologists in Iraq over the last sixty years tell us much about the earliest civilization known to man, that of the Sumerians, which existed as far back as the third millennium B.C. The Sumerians, happily for us, left behind them very detailed descriptions, drawings, and accounts of all the important matters in their lives. One of the things preserved for us out of this page from long ago is a map of the ancient Sumerian city of Nippur, which, around 3400 B.C., was a center of religion and culture in the southern part of Mesopotamia. What look like scratches of some erratic bird etched into a piece of clay tablet are actually figures written in a script known as cuneiform, a wedge-shaped writing used by these ancient peoples. On a map of clay are indicated the names of rivers, canals, gates, temples, and parks in this city of the past.

Of course the Sumerians needed some method of keeping their accounts, their records of business transactions. Shaping clay from the riverbanks into tablets and using a pen or a stylus made from the wild reeds at the river's edge, they inscribed onto the half-dried surface pictures of what they wished to record. A merchant who was about to deliver five pounds of wheat to a customer and wished to present a bill would draw a bundle of wheat and next to it five circles. Dried in the sun, the tablets became so hard that they were

An ancient record of a farmer's taxes on a Babylonian clay tablet, VII Century B.C. (c. 617).

able to survive over 5,000 years, and so we are able to look at them and study them today.

Because the characters used represented sounds, this writing evolved into what we call *phonics,* and was used by the Babylonians and the Assyrians after them. These tablets are in fact books, on which was recorded the entire literary creativeness of the Sumerians. Their subject matter ranges over religion, economics, history, medicine, music, philosophy, aspects of social life, and a variety of other topics. These tablets have made it possible for modern scholars to penetrate deeply into the heart and soul of this most ancient people. Before the days of the Romans, the Greeks, the Phoenicians, the Babylonians, and even the Egyptians, it was the Sumerians who bequeathed to us their civilization.

Who were the Sumerians, and from where did they come? Earlier settlers had lived in this part of the world during the Stone Age, before history was recorded in any way. The people lived in caves and rock shelters in the hilly northern part of the country, and eventually were able to develop an agricultural way of life, for the land they dwelt on was rich and fruitful.

Archaeologists believe that the Sumerians, a non-Semitic, black-haired people, may have come about 4000 B.C. from the Iranian highlands to the east and northeast. Until quite recently little was known about them, but now every turn of the spade adds a new page to the background of ancient Mesopotamia's history, and today we really know more about them than about most of the other peoples of the ancient Middle East. We no longer think that all art, science, religion, literature, mathematics, astronomy and architecture, or the arch, the plow, the wheel, writing, and even the art of war must be attributed to the Romans and the Greeks, for they in their turn had taken them from the Lydians, Cretans, Hittites, Phoenicians, Babylonians, Assyrians or Egyptians. But these marks of civilization stem even farther back—from the inventive and energetic people of ancient Sumer.

Some people believed that in very early times the head of the Persian Gulf was far to the north of its present site, and that the entire marsh area, the southern part of Iraq today, was then completely submerged. More recently it has been thought that part of the Arabian Gulf was once land. An ancient map shows us that Iraq, as late as A.D. 22, was still different from what it is today. The sites of cities north of the capital were located directly on the Tigris, but those to the south were close to, but not actually on, the Euphrates. Later, the actual course of the river changed and this forced inhabitants of the towns along its banks to move elsewhere. Eventually the earlier towns and cities fell into ruin.

If we were to take a field trip among the treasures of Iraq's past, we would start in the southern city of Basra on the Shatt-al-Arab, and strike north some hundred miles along the old course of the Euphrates to Abu Shahrein, site of the ancient city of Eridu. This holy city of the Sumerians is said to be their oldest, perhaps the first community that emerged from the overwhelming water of the great flood. People lived there 5,000 years ago, working in their shops, planting and irrigating their gardens, going to school, writing their

The excavations on the site of Eridu revealed a city of temples and cloisters. Here is a series of views of the principal shrines, superimposed on one another in 18 successive building levels, the latest of which was the ziggurat, or stepped tower, of the city.

thoughts on clay tablets, and worshiping their favorite gods. On what is now but a desolate waste of sand once stood impressive temples and cloisters, where priests prayed in seclusion or gathered together for a religious ceremony. There were shrines, curiously built one on top of another, and these ziggurats, or step towers as they were called, were an important part of the temple in those days, much as a steeple of a church or a minaret of a mosque is today. The temples were dedicated to Enki, lord of wisdom and foresight and the chief god of the city.

In those far-off days temples were the chief centers of activity. Business was conducted in their rooms, school was held there, laws were handed down, and water distributed. There were even shops for arts and crafts in them.

Twenty miles north of Eridu was once the great city of Ur, the Chaldean home of Abraham. A familiar name to readers of the Bible, he is referred to as Prophet Abraham in the Koran, the Moslem holy book. It is this same Abraham who gave up his life in a settled, cultured community to follow the call of God, and who became the father of the Hebrews.

The waste of rubble that is Ur today was in Abraham's day fortified, like all ancient cities. It spread over an area of about four square miles. Perhaps there was a harbor and a quay for shipping—if the assumption is true that in those days the waters of the gulf extended far to the north of where they are today. Houses then were not much different from those we might see in a small Iraqi town today—sometimes two stories high and built of sun-dried brick around an open court. The rooms consisted of kitchen, reception hall, washroom, an altar for worship, and a burial vault under the floor of the main rooms. Doorways were open arches, since wood was scarce. Roofs were flat and probably often used for sleeping, just as they are today.

Even the daily life of these ancient people would be familiar to us. There were farmers among them, breeders of cattle, boatmen and fishermen, merchants and craftsmen. They kept the same domestic animals, used much the same sort of furniture, and frequented the same kind of souk as do their descendants today.

It is possible for archaeologists to reconstruct the towns, houses, and temples of the past with ever greater accuracy, for discovery is a continuous thing, and new findings from Iraq are constantly gathered and collected in the museums of the world to be studied by all who are fascinated by the history of the past. This is how we are able to know with reasonable certainty about, for example, the Sumerian king who with his queen and guards and chambermaids was buried in the royal tomb some 2,600 years before Christ. Within the brick and limestone chambers of their tomb were placed the royal pair's most valuable possessions. Besides furniture, there were two enormous harps shaped like the head of a bull, heavily inlaid and decorated with gold, mother-of-pearl, and lapis lazuli. One of these harps can be seen at the Iraqi Museum in Baghdad, the other

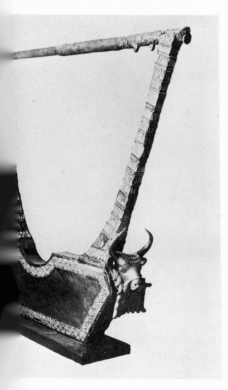

Left: *Harp with bull's head of pure gold from the royal tombs of the Chaldeans in Ur. (c. 2600* B.C.*) Below: Iraqi necklace.*

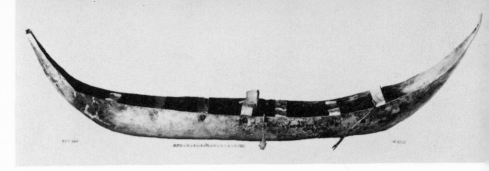

Boat taken from the tomb of a Sumerian king.

is in the United States at the Museum of the University of Pennsylvania at Philadelphia. Also buried with them were personal jewelry, headdresses and necklaces of gold, and daggers exquisitely ornamented with filigree. Most important of all to the pair was a small boat, much like the *balam* of today, in which they would be borne on their journey to the other world.

On the railway timetables now Ur is but a tiny stop called Tell al-Muqayyar, halfway between Baghdad and Basra. Larsa, the Antioch of the Bible, is another ancient city that now only exists in the memory. Here too was a temple with imposing ziggurat dedicated to Shamash, the sun god, and here too many objects of interest were dug out from the rubble-covered tombs that had lain buried beneath the sand for countless centuries. Still farther north lay the city of Uruk, a center of religion and learning known as Erech in the Bible. It was fortified by Gilgamesh, one of its kings whose name is forever glorified in an Akkadian epic poem that also describes the Great Flood and an ark, their earliest mention in literature, predating the Old Testament. In one version of this poem, the Sumerian counterpart of the biblical Noah is named Utnapishtim and the ark came to rest, not on Mt. Ararat, but on Mt. Nisir in the north of Iraq. Beautiful pottery, painted vessels, colored mosaics of baked clay set in patterns that look like a Persian carpet, have been found in what were the cities of Fara, Adab, Isin, Nippur and Borsippa. In temple rooms used for schools and libraries of these communities were stacked clay tablet on clay tablet covering a multitude of different subjects: medicine, agriculture, horticulture, philosophy, wise sayings, fables, and religion.

In those far-off times these Sumerian cities were, with the villages that surrounded them, small independent city states ruled by a king whose kingship came, the inhabitants believed, from heaven. Each king was aided by a group of elders and leading men of the community, much like the privy council of more modern days. Rivalry between these states was inevitable, and in the year 2300 B.C. the first world empire was created by Sargon of Akkad, a Semite who overcame the Sumerians and welded these separate states into a unit. He was later able to extend his domain west as far as the Mediterranean. The Akkadian kings who followed him are known as great organizers and builders, relinquishing their nomadic habits and adopting much from the civilization they had conquered.

Two hundred years later the Amorites, another Semitic people

Gudea, ruler of Lagash, who dedicated this stone statue of himself to a Sumerian god, "To whom life has been given." (c. 2050 B.C.)

from Arabia, overran the Akkadian territory and adopted the writings, literature, religion, science, and customs of the Sumerians. From this fusion came two great peoples: the Babylonians, who occupied the middle of the valley around Babylon, their capital, and the Assyrians, in the north, centered in their cities of Ashur and Nineveh. ". . . and the beginning of his kingdom was Babel and Erech and Accad . . ." says the Bible, thus recording the primitive origin of the ancient city of Babylon, whose name means "Gate of God." By 1800 B.C. it was the capital of a vast empire, a seat of power, and the center of the ancient world. Its greatest period was under Hammurabi, who codified the laws of the day and whose name has come down to us for this achievement. He ruled from 1792 to 1750 B.C.

To the north lie the rolling hills where the Assyrians once ruled. They enjoyed a cool climate, healthful altitude, and considerable mineral wealth. Excellent stone and fine marble went into the building of the beautiful palaces of mighty kings: Sennacherib, Ashurbanipal, and Sargon. And because these palaces were built of these sturdy materials instead of the mud and dried brick used by the Babylonians, more of their remains have lasted through the ages. In museums today we can see the great achievements of the Assyrians portrayed on the richly ornamented bas-reliefs that decorated the walls of these palaces. Though of course based on the Sumerian and Babylonian cultures that preceded it, Assyrian civilization had a definite character of its own. These men of the north were bellicose, in constant battle with Sumer, Akkad, and later the closely related Babylonians. The empire extended, at its height, all the way to Egypt on one side and the highlands of Persia on the other, and after the thirteenth century B.C. the Assyrians were masters of all the Near East. Because of their love of waging war and their administrative ability, they are known in the history books as "the Romans of the East."

These people worshiped the god Ashur, considering him the father of all gods and goddesses, the god of heaven and the entire universe. The first capital was named Ashur after him, and was erected

Bronze head of Sargon the Great, King of Akkad. (c. 2400 B.C.)

on a spot some two hundred miles to the north of Babylon. Here was the birthplace of the Assyrian nation, and under its sacred soil its kings were buried.

Built on the banks of the Tigris, Ashur, it is believed, was founded soon after the occurrence of the great flood. Throughout its history the city was the empire's religious center. The modern town of Shar-qat, some sixty miles south of Mosul, comes closest to the vast ruins that are what remain of Ashur today.

Forty miles north of Ashur on the eastern bank of the Tigris, stood Nimrud, called Calah in the Bible. The city was built on a square, surrounded by a well-fortified wall. A tall obelisk, which stood in the huge open courtyard of the palace, gives us much information about Nimrud. This palace overlooked the river, and was built by Ashurnasirpal II, ruler of Assyria from 884 to 859 B.C. According to the obelisk, the palace was built by prisoners of war. When it was completed a lavish banquet was held in celebration, to which were invited not only notables from throughout the empire but all the inhabitants of the city.

The doors of the huge throne room, which opened onto the courtyard, were flanked by colossal alabaster figures of winged lions with human heads. Two of these stone figures can be seen in New York's Metropolitan Museum. The head is said to represent intellect and wisdom, the lion's body strength, and the eagle's wings rapidity of motion.

Bas-reliefs depicting the daily life of the court decorated the outer face of this great hall. There is one scene that shows horse-drawn chariots; another, the hunting of animals; while a third portrays the king, surrounded by ministers, with attendants in train.

As in all cities of the time, the temple was an important feature of the royal palace. Nimrud, the military capital of the empire, was no exception, and the temple stood at the palace's northwest corner, topped by its ziggurat.

Twenty miles farther to the north is all that is left of Nineveh, a city that in the eighth century B.C. became the capital of the Assyrian Empire. At that time it surpassed even Babylon in wealth and magnificence.

Excavations begun a little over a century ago have yielded many valuable objects and much information about the ancient history of Mesopotamia. Even more outstanding than the unearthing of pottery, cylinder seals, winged bulls and lions of stone, and bas-reliefs was the discovery of the library of Ashurbanipal that lay buried in the ruins of his palace at Nineveh. Here hundreds of priceless clay tablets were found—books, in effect—with an index that listed them all and showed the location of each. Many of the tablets were on religious subjects; some dealt with magic, others with medicine or astronomy, and one was a version of the Gilgamesh epic, with its account of the Deluge and a reference to the ark.

Today Nineveh is known as Tell Kouyunjik, or "small hill." It is a favorite place for school children to picnic; they sit on the top of the tell overlooking the little River Khosar as it winds, snakelike, down the valley to join the Tigris half a mile away. The scene the children look at is as busy as in ancient times, but there is no royal barge or chariot speeding the king on his way, no parade of soldiers with battering-ram on their way to war, no procession of weary captives from Samaria or Syria. Today the children look down on women and girls from neighboring villages washing the linen in the river, beating it with pieces of wood to get out the dirt; perhaps they see a shepherd driving his sheep to water.

A little beyond the river stands a mosque, its minaret high against the sky. This is the village of Nebi Yunus, where, it is believed, lies the tomb of Jonah, who was tested in the body of the whale and was sent by God to preach to the sinful people of Nineveh. Every year hundreds of Christians, Moslems, and Jews make the journey to visit his tomb.

Northeast of Nineveh is the site of a once great city called Dur Sharrukin, where Sargon II built himself a summer palace in 721 B.C. This discovery of the archaeologists gave the world its first illumination of the land and culture of ancient Assyria. Besides the seven-story ziggurat and some beautiful and lavishly decorated blue-glazed brickwork, they uncovered an inscription which reads: "For me, Sargon, who dwells in that place, may he [he is talking of the god Ashur] decree as my destiny long life, health of body, joy of heart, and brightness of soul." But the god could not have listened to this prayer, for Sargon was killed in battle a short two years later—and his palace crumbled into ruins.

In 612 B.C., nearly a century later, the Assyrian Empire itself fell. The Babylonians from the south, whose star was once more rising, and the Medes, forerunners of the Persians, jointly struck down the already faltering Assyria. A treaty was signed between the Medes and the Babylonians; the pact was sealed by the marriage of a Median princess to the young Babylonian king, Nebuchadnezzar.

The once great city of Nineveh was burned to the ground.

As the power of Ashur and Nineveh waned, the star of Babylon ascended once again, and it was during the height of the second great Babylonian dynasty that the city was rebuilt by King Nebuchadnezzar. It was a most beautiful city that he created, with fortified walls, magnificent palaces, and lofty temples. The streets were paved. But while Babylon became a center of wisdom, a place of much commerce and manufacturing, it was also a land of captivity to the hun-

Hanging Gardens on the roofs of Nebuchadnezzar's palace in Babylon.

dreds of Hebrews who had lived there in bondage for over fifty years. As generation of them followed generation, some, to be sure, were attracted by the luxury and wealth of the city and instead of returning to Palestine, their promised land, when this was allowed them at a later date, they adopted Babylon as their own. But Babylon remained to the prophets of the Hebrews what Rome was to John in the Apocalypse—a city of the greatest worldliness, sensuality, and vice.

But it must have been a beautiful city, located, as Herodotus tells us, on both sides of the Euphrates and connected by a stone bridge— the first that we know about. Built on a square pattern, its streets were wide enough for two chariots drawn by four horses to pass each other. The walls were high, and the space between them was cultivated to provide food for the citizens in case of siege. Guards patrolled the walls and watchtowers, which were spaced every 160 feet. There were two fortresses, one in each half of the city, and in one of them was the royal palace, enclosed by a massive wall. Extensive in area, it was lavishly decorated, enameled in fine brick relief. High above arched, vaulted stone structures were the terraced gardens of the palace—the famed Hanging Gardens of Babylon. Built by Nebuchadnezzar for his Median wife Amytas so that she would not miss her mountain home, these gardens were considered by the Greeks as one of the seven wonders of the ancient world. This masterpiece of engineering and technical planning had a continuous supply of water, pumped from a well with a triple shaft, for the many varieties of trees and plants brought from every corner of the vast empire. Renown for the beauty of the hanging gardens has lasted through the ages.

The other half of the city contained the temple, with its ziggurat overlooking the city and the surrounding fields. This was the "tower of Babel," and the "babel of tongues" referred to in the Bible were the languages spoken by Akkadians, Amorites, Aramaeans, Elamites, Kassites, and others who all lived within the walls of the city of Babylon. The temple itself was square and consisted of eight towers, one on top of another. The top of the ziggurat was reached by way of a spiral staircase encircling the outside. There were seats halfway up, for those who became tired. In those ancient days a great temple stood on the topmost tower, and in it were a golden table and a richly covered couch, ready for the gods to use.

The yearly climax of temple worship came in the month of Nisan (April), and marked the festival of the new year. All gathered in the city to celebrate. "Processional Way," a walled road built especially for this purpose, was decorated for the occasion. Amid the shouts and excitement of the crowd, priests carried their gods along the road and through the Gate of Ishtar, which led from the temple to the palace.

Herodotus was fascinated not only by the actual appearance of this fabulous metropolis, but also by the great fertility of the surrounding countryside. Here is his description of Babylonia: "Of all the countries that we know there is none that is so fruitful in grain. It makes no pretension indeed of growing the fig, the olive, the vine, or any other tree of the kind; but in grain it is so fruitful as to yield commonly two-hundredfold." Today, because of the broken-down irrigation system and archaic methods still being used, the land yields only between thirty- and forty-fold.

In this center of wealth and cultural patronage, of literature, art, codes of law, astronomy, and mathematics, learning was a byword. Due to the laws codified by Hammurabi, justice ruled. These laws, inscribed on a black-diorite stele, can be seen now in the Louvre museum in Paris. They deal with a diversity of matters: family relations, divorce, agriculture, slavery, and inheritance. The state had replaced the individual as the bestower of justice. Mathematics derived from the fusion of the Sumerian sexagesimal and the Semitic decimal system. Increased knowledge of the heavens and the stars that moved therein made astronomy an exact science.

What happened in this giant empire, which at one time reached as far west as Egypt, to cause its collapse? After the death of Nebuchadnezzar, in 562 B.C., Nabonidus, of a different royal line, came to the throne. This was a good man, a scholar who loved peace and the antiquities that surrounded him. But he was a poor politician, utterly uninterested in catering to the priests and soldiers who filled his court. So they came to hate him. His neglect of the affairs of state and the widening schisms dividing his people caused the gradual decline of his empire and made possible its defeat by Cyrus of Persia in the year 539 B.C. when Nabonidus' son was prince and regent. It was this son, Belshazzar, who saw the writing on the wall at the time of the prophet Daniel. And what was begun by the sword was ended by nature when the Euphrates River changed its course to westward, leaving the once mighty city of Babylon without water in the arid desert.

Today, some seventy miles to the south of Baghdad, a wooden

sign sticks up out of the sand. The letters that spell Babylon can hardly be deciphered through the film of dust and sand that covers it. The Gate of Ishtar, outlined against the skyline, faces the remains of the terraces that once supported the Hanging Gardens. Little of the past remains to mark this once luxuriant and brightly colored spot. Only the stone Lion of Babylon stands guard over what once was Nebuchadnezzar's palace.

The Gate of Ishtar.

4

Once a Christian Country

WHEN AT LAST the Assyrian capital of Nineveh was crushed in 612 B.C. and the second period of the Babylonians' greatness collapsed some seventy years later, an illustrious chapter in the history of Mesopotamia came to an end. The warlike kings who had shaped the destiny of the ancient world had gone forever. The land was instead reduced to the status of a mere province, under the rule of foreign powers based outside its borders. This state of affairs was a pattern that persisted for many centuries. For hundreds of years Mesopotamia was crossed and recrossed by kings, emperors, military leaders, by armies, bands of prisoners, by adventurers and traders. Some came from the east across the mountains, others were from the west and that land beyond the desert and close to the sea. All competed, in war and in peace, for this land between the two great rivers, and all sought to trade with the fabulous Orient. All took part in the destruction. Many took part in the rebuilding.

The first of the conquerors was Cyrus the Persian, in 539 B.C. Instead of razing the old capital, Babylon—a usual practice of conquerors—he admired it to the point of making it his own winter capital. Though a Zoroastrian himself, he visited the Babylonians' temple and even offered sacrifices to their gods. The name of Cyrus has gone down in history as one of the greatest of monarchs, for in no way was he a ruthless despot. He spared the lives of those whose lands he overran. He permitted the exiled Jews to return to Jerusalem, there to rebuild the temple. And it was Cyrus who made it possible for those Persian kings who followed him to unite Southwest Asia into one well-organized empire. One of the chief contributions to this end was the building of a road stretching from Sardis in Asia Minor to Susa, Persia's capital. Thus were all parts of the empire accessible one to another. This highway was known as the Royal Road, and along it some hundred years later marched the ill-fated ten thousand, the Greek mercenary soldiers who, under a Persian prince, were on their way to Babylon to attempt the overthrow of the ruling dynasty. Their march down the Euphrates and their retreat back up the Tigris is reported for posterity in the fifth century B.C. by the Greek historian Xenophon. He was an eyewitness to the dismal failure of this mission, and helped his countrymen in their retreat. Incidentally, this was the first Western military expedition to fight on Eastern soil.

The power and the glory that was Persia's fell in turn when again the plains of the river valley saw a display of great military might under the young Macedonian, Alexander. A decisive battle was fought by him against Darius III in 331 B.C. at Arbela, about forty miles from what is now Mosul. This battle marked the beginning of the rise of the West and the decline of Eastern power in this area. At the height of his strength, Alexander the Great's empire stretched as far as the Indus River, in what is Pakistan today. Like Cyrus before him, the Grecian conqueror was captivated by the beauty of Babylon, and he too made it the capital of his Eastern territories. He was at last realizing a long-held dream for the unification of East and West into one world, based on absolute equality and with individual freedom and human rights regardless of religion, race, or color. To this end Alexander encouraged his men to marry Eastern women, and set the example by his own marriage to Roxana, a beautiful Persian princess. He built many cities and populated them with Greeks so that Greek civilization would spread throughout the region through personal contact and through trade. Unhappily, he did not live long enough to witness the development of the Hellenistic period and the growth of the seeds he planted, for he died at the age of thirty-two in 323 B.C.

After the death of Alexander his vast empire was divided up into a number of kingdoms presided over by his erstwhile generals. Mesopotamia fell to Seleucus, who did not appreciate the city of Babylon in the same way. Instead he built a new capital on the banks of the Tigris some twenty miles south of what is now Baghdad, and he named it Seleucia. This city, situated on the route between India and the Persian Gulf, became important as a new center of culture and commerce.

But in nearby Persia a renewed spirit of nationalism was growing in strength. By 140 B.C. the Persians were once again a powerful people, able to bring the Greek Seleucid dynasty to an end. This conquest marks the beginning of the new Persian Parthian Empire, whose capital, Ctesiphon, was built on the Tigris opposite Seleucia. Today Ctesiphon is in ruins, referred to as *taqi Kisra*, but its great arch remains as a testament to its magnificence.

The Parthian kings, whose rule was distinguished by the tolerance shown peoples of differing religions and races, organized their vast empire into small states and settlements. Each was governed by its native ruler and managed its own affairs, while paying taxes directly to the Parthian "king of kings," as he was called. Some of these small states, located on the Syrian-Mesopotamian frontiers, rose to considerable importance. This was particularly the case during the long series of wars between the increasingly powerful Romans and the lands to the east. The Romans had supplanted the Greeks as major proponents of Western influence, and were gradually building up a great Eastern Roman Empire in addition to their sprawling empire of the West.

This struggle between East and West began about 44 B.C., the year Caesar was assassinated, and lasted for several hundred years and through the Arab occupation. For the most part the Euphrates marked the boundary between lands ruled by Persia and those ruled by Byzantium, as the Eastern Roman Empire was called. The ruins of fortress cities such as Harran, Edessa (Urfa), Nisibin, Amida (Diyarbekir), Dara, and Hatra show signs even today of this warfare. Mesopotamia, generally speaking, in the possession of Persia to the south and the Byzantines to the north, became once more a region of contention between these two giant forces. People went about their business filled with confusion and despair, for they were never sure that they would wake up the next day governed by the same ruler as the night before. Cities, towns, and villages were constantly under attack. In the north, the streets swarmed with strangely

The Arch of Ctesiphon.

clad soldiers who spoke many tongues and came from all corners of the far-flung Roman Empire. There were Goths, Moors, Vandals, Greeks, Syrians, and Armenians. Some were slaves, others were freedmen. Some were pagan, Magians, worshipers of mysterious cults; and there were Jews. But within the Roman Empire all traveled along well-constructed open roads on which no passport was necessary.

Thus whatever was newsworthy was known to many, for travelers on these roads told of what went on beyond the Euphrates and the border of Syria. It was in this way that the people of Mesopotamia heard of a man named Jesus. He lived in Palestine and, it was said, performed miracles.

A nobleman from Hatra, II Century A.D.

The time was ripe, for morale was low.

By the beginning of the third century Christianity was widespread. Many churches were built to the new faith, some even on Mesopotamia's borders. Only recently one was unearthed in Syria, at Dura Europus on the banks of the Euphrates. The ruins are of a church dating back to A.D. 232, making it one of the earliest Christian churches ever discovered. (It, in turn, had been built over the ruins of an even earlier synagogue.)

In A.D. 226 the Parthian Persians were replaced by the Sassanian Persians. The new kings placed no obstacles in the way of the Christian religion, and few changes were made in the organization of the vast new territory under their rule. In Rome, however, it wasn't until A.D. 313, in the Edict of Milan, that the Emperor Constantine ended the years of persecution. It was this ruler who made Byzantium, which he named Constantinople, the capital of the Eastern Roman Empire.

By the fourth century Christianity was the official religion of the Byzantine Empire. But the Persians living in Mesopotamia were hostile to the Byzantine Christians, whom their Magian priests accused of being sympathetic with the Roman Christians. As a result several waves of persecution took place, the most serious being in the second half of the fourth century, when as many as 16,000 Christians suffered martyrdom. Heavy taxation was levied on those fortunate enough to survive. Nevertheless Christianity flourished, and the number of converts increased among many Persian officials, and even among the princes and princesses.

Up to the fifth century the Christians of Mesopotamia had formed one community, which was known as the Church of the East. We know of this church now as the Eastern Orthodox Church, to which Greeks, Russians, and others belong. Before the end of the fifth century, however, a religious schism occurred in Constantinople concerning the human and divine natures of Christ. This resulted in the church dividing into two: one sect, the Nestorians, believed that the human and divine natures were joined in perfect action within Jesus Christ, but not in the unity of a single individual. The other sect, the Monophysites, or Jacobites, claimed that the human and divine constituted but one nature altogether. This schism caused a number of Greek scholars, who were Christians, to leave Constantinople to make new homes for themselves in Mesopotamia and Persia. There they joined others like them, becoming teachers in the schools and colleges of Edessa, Nisibin, Ctesiphon, and Seleucia. Some entered the many monasteries which by this time were flourishing in the region, particularly to the north and northwest. There were monasteries, or convents, for women as well as men.

The monasteries were seldom built in towns or cities, but were rather found on the plains, deserts, or mountain peaks. All were fortified against attack by robbers or raids by unfriendly tribes. All were near some sort of water supply, either from river, mountain spring, oasis, or well. Some of these springs were thought to have healing powers, and the sick came from all over the country to drink from the waters, or bathe in them. Many of the monasteries were constructed with beautiful domes so that they could be seen from afar, a beacon for travelers seeking sanctuary. Inside, precious art objects of gold and silver could be seen, such as fine candlesticks used for the burning of incense or wax candles during religious ceremonies.

Monks spent active, well-disciplined lives in seclusion in their *qallaya,* or cell. These cells were often actually hewn out of the mountainside, or built apart from the main building. It was not unusual for a monastery to contain as many as a thousand of these cells. The monks lived according to the rules of their order regarding prayer, fasting, study, and meditation, and they also fulfilled various duties connected with maintaining the establishment and housing and feeding large numbers of guests. All within the walls were summoned to meals or prayer by the striking of a heavy bell, or *naqus,* with a hammer. Libraries were an important part of each monastery, containing large numbers of manuscripts on such subjects as theology, philosophy, medicine, chemistry, and astronomy. The monks added continually to this storehouse of treasures by spending much of their time writing, translating, and transcribing into Syriac the books written by the Greeks. It was between the fourth and seventh centuries

The Deir mar Sheikh Matti Monastery.

that these monasteries, and Christianity as a whole, reached their peak in this region. In A.D. 631 a Nestorian Christian mission from Mesopotamia actually made its way to China. Today we can see there the stele of Sian, which bears an inscription both in Chinese and Syriac that lists the names of the sixty-seven missionaries from that voyage.

There is no doubt that the monasteries provided the means for preserving Greek philosophy and science, in fact the entire richness and wealth of the Greek heritage, which might otherwise have been lost to us. Through the monks' faithfulness in copying and transcribing Greek manuscripts, the Hellenic civilization passed from Greece and her empire to the Syriac-speaking communities, thence to the Arab world of Islam, and finally to the Romans and the Latin-instructed schools of western Europe.

At this period of history, when the East and West were battling for control of Mesopotamia and when the monks in their monasteries were living as serenely as possible in those troubled times, a voice was heard from the far-off desert of Arabia. The voice belonged to a man named Mohammed, who was unknown to the world. He and his disciples called on the Persian "king of kings" to believe with them in Allah, the one and only God, and to fight the *jihad*, or holy war, in his name. The echo of Mohammed's voice was heard throughout the Middle East, and its reverberation did not stop until the giant Persian Empire toppled and was overcome in A.D. 637. Four years after this date all of Mesopotamia became a part of the Arab domain, and Islam its religion.

❖ 5 ❖

The Moslem Caliphate

By THE BEGINNING of the seventh century A.D., conflict had greatly weakened, both externally and internally, the two giant empires of Persia in the East and Byzantium, the Eastern Roman Empire, in the West. Thus it was possible for the fresh and vigorous Semitic Arabs to push both powers out of the Arabian peninsula. The Arabs did more: they were able to take from the Persians and Romans the lower part of the Fertile Crescent, which is now Iraq.

It was in eastern Arabia, in the tiny town of Mecca, that Mohammed, a simple and illiterate Bedouin, was born in A.D. 570. At first a tender of sheep, Mohammed became a driver for caravans of camels owned by wealthy merchants traveling between Mecca and Syria. In the course of these journeys Mohammed spoke to many— to Jew and to Christian as well as pagan. He learned much about their beliefs, their religion, their holy books. The infinite quiet of the desert gave him the chance to mull over his own ideas, and finally to develop a faith which he began to preach to his own divided and pagan people. Like the Christians and Jews, he believed in the one supreme God, whom he called Allah, and he was convinced that he, Mohammed, spoke with the voice of Allah. His influence grew, and when the leaders of Mecca moved against him in 622, he was forced to flee with a few of his followers to Medina, some 300 miles to the north, where he was enthusiastically received. This flight, or *hegira,* which is the Arab word, became the year 1 of the Moslem era. Instead of marking the years as we do, A.D. (Anno Domini) "in the year of our Lord," the Arabs write A.H., Anno Hegira.

The Hegira became a turning point in man's history. This third great monotheistic religious movement came about through Mohammed's courage and faith in his mission. He called this religion Islam, meaning submission to the will of God. With it came also a political revolution, as the nomadic desert tribes and the petty Arab states all came together for the first time under the control of Mohammed and the caliphs who followed him.

The main profession of this new belief, known as *shahada,* lay in the submission to and the acceptance of the will of God and his statutes. In his role as God's messenger (this was a basic tenet of the faith), Mohammed felt it was necessary to regulate and govern not only the principles but the entire way of life of the Moslem people. He laid down five rules of worship for his followers: the recital of the creed, the five daily prayers, the giving of tithes to the poor, the fasting one month a year during Ramadan, and one pilgrimage to Mecca. The community as a whole was to make up the brotherhood of this new religion, which was to have no priesthood and no leadership other than Mohammed. Koran, which means "recitation of the word of God," is the name Mohammed gave to his teachings, which were, he believed and taught his followers, dictated to him by God through the angel Gabriel. Compiled as a book after his death, the Koran contains many stories familiar to readers of the Bible; it tells of Adam, Noah, Abraham, and others, and it is in many ways an echo of the Judaeo-Christian religion.

Christians in Iraq, who had looked on their Persian masters as foreigners, welcomed the conquering Moslems, feeling toward them a kinship as fellow Semites. So the doors of the churches and monasteries were opened wide to the new arrivals. Like the Christians, Moslems believed in a Day of Judgment and in reward and punishment in the afterlife, and they in turn respected the Christians and their leaders. Did it not say in the Koran: ". . . and thou shalt certainly find to be nearest in affection to those who say 'we are Christian.' This is because some of them are priests and monks, and because they are free from pride."

The caliphs—the very word means "a successor"—who followed after Mohammed's death, ruled Iraq from 632 to 1258, when they were overthrown by the Mongols. The caliphate can be divided into three groups: the Orthodox caliphate; the Ommiad; and the Abbasside—a total of fifty-five caliphs. These princes carried the Prophet's message far beyond the Arabian peninsula. It was not only religious zeal spurring them on; economic necessity added impetus to the drive toward more fertile regions and an easier and more luxurious way of life. And so, in less than one hundred years, the Moslem occupation reached westward to North Africa, Spain, and the south of France, and eastward to the Indus River and the confines of China. The struggle between the Byzantine emperors of Constantinople and the caliphs of Baghdad was waged over land and sea, and it was a bitter, lengthy, hard-fought war that was decided finally in the tenth century A.D. in favor of the Arabs (for a while).

As was to be expected, there were bitter struggles between rivals for the caliphate. A civil war had broken out. Othman, the third caliph, had died and left no heir. The dispute lay between Imam Ali, the fourth caliph, who was also the son-in-law of the Prophet and governor of Syria, and Muawiya, the head of the opposition party. Muawiya's party was later known as the Sunni, an important faction in the history of Iraq still existing today as a strong religious group, particularly in the north. Muawiya was supported by the people of Syria, and Ali therefore was forced to flee to Iraq, which backed up his claim in turn. There he founded the Shiite movement; its followers make up half the population of Iraq today and are found in the south. When Ali was pursued by his rival, a full-scale battle followed, during which he was murdered. His son Hussein continued the fight, only to be killed in his turn, as was the third son. The tombs of the three murdered princes have become little meccas, where thousands of pilgrims come to pay homage; the faithful hope that their own remains may one day rest in one of these holy places.

The victorious Muawiya had settled in Syria and made the ancient city of Damascus his capital. The rulers of the city came to be known as the Ommiad caliphs, and it was under their rule that the Moslem Empire achieved its greatest expansion. Nevertheless Iraq, with her Shiite sympathizers, remained a thorn in the side of Damascus and, capitalizing on revolts and open insurrection taking place elsewhere, was the cause of the final downfall of the empire. In 750 the Ommiad caliphate passed from Damascus, Syria, to Iraq, to be governed by the Abbasside dynasty (descending from Abbas, an uncle of Mohammed).

The period of the Abbasside caliphate is known in history as the Arabs' Golden Age. It was an era of magnificence and splendor, with Baghdad, a cosmopolitan and international center of the medieval world, as its capital. It lasted from A.D. 750 to 1258, and in all there numbered thirty-seven caliphs. We can see in the museums of today the pictures, drawings, sketches, tapestries, and descriptions in beautiful Arabian calligraphy portraying the life of the time.

From records that have come down to us we know that the caliph was the head of a theocratic state, holding both temporal and spiritual authority as the head of church and state as the successor to the Prophet. Sometimes the caliph is shown surrounded by members of his family, by viziers and ministers, by advisers and high government officials. In another tableau the head of state is receiving foreign envoys and ambassadors from other lands with great pomp and ceremony. We can see the caliph on the battlefield commanding troops, or walking the streets of Baghdad disguised as a commoner in order to see the real condition of his city and hear the complaints of his people against injustice. One scene shows him touring the streets to choose a site for a hospital; others are of colorful ceremonies dedicating a school, college, or mosque. In another picture the caliph is surrounded by scholars and learned men, who are hotly discussing the ideas and problems of the times.

Scenes from *The Arabian Nights,* so brilliantly immortalized by the story teller Scheherazade, reveal the gay and luxurious city life that was adopted by the Arabs from the conquered Persians after abandoning the simplicity of the desert. The tale of Sinbad the sailor starts out: "There lived in the city of Baghdad, during the reign of the Commander of the Faithful, Harun al-Rashid . . ." and it was during his reign that the zenith of the Golden Age was reached. Even Tennyson wrote of the city: "A goodly place, a goodly time . . . For it was in the golden prime of good Harun al-Rashid." The country was highly prosperous, its inhabitants enjoying a high standard of living. The royal palace occupied one third of the city, with many annexes for servants, the harem, the slaves, and court functionaries. The other great monarch of the age was Charlemagne, ruler of the Franks, and it is said that he and Harun exchanged gifts of great worth. Among those sent westward by Harun were an elephant, a chessboard, a water clock considered one of the marvels of the day, and many costly fabrics and perfumes.

It is said that Zubayda, Harun's wife and also his cousin, would not permit any vessel at her table that was not of gold, of silver, or studded with jewels. She was the first woman to use cloth with many ornaments on it, and she even introduced the wearing of painted fabrics. She wore shoes of silver, sandalwood, and ebony, many of them rich with precious stones. And when she made her pilgrimage to Mecca, she furnished the holy city with water brought from thirty miles away. Later, she built wells and cisterns along the 900-mile route taken by the pilgrims from Iraq to Hejaz, at a cost of what was believed to be about three million dinars.

The women of the royal household, and in fact all women of the Abbasside period, enjoyed a relatively high degree of freedom, for Moslem law gave them full legal rights and assured them of economic independence. Actually at this time women did not go veiled, nor were they secluded, but appeared publicly in the company of men. Many even went to war, fighting bravely beside their men. There were some who commanded troops. Others rose to prominent positions, wielding great influence in the affairs of state. A large number distinguished themselves as scholars, especially in the performance of Moslem religious functions. Others lectured in the university, composed poetry, and competed with men generally in various literary pursuits. Quite a few won fame as singers and musicians. At the end of the Abbasside dynasty, however, the women of the wealthier classes were secluded, so that they could be better protected, and they wore the veil to distinguish them from the female slaves.

Harun's death in A.D. 809 caused a civil war between factions led by his two sons. Amin, favored by the Arab party at court, assumed office but was later murdered by the followers of Mamun, the other son, whose accession was desired by the Persian elements in Baghdad. Weary months of anarchy and bloodshed racked the region before Amin's death and the succession of his brother.

The eighth caliph to rule in Baghdad was Mutasim, another son of Harun, whose mother was a Turkish slave. Because at this time the Persian influence at court was very strong, Mutasim surrounded himself with a Turkish bodyguard. However, the unpopularity of these foreigners created such an impossible situation that the caliph was forced to leave the city. He built himself another capital, on the left bank of the Tigris some seventy miles to the northwest. It was called Samarra, or in Arabic *Surra-man ra'* which means "happy is he who sees it." Though the city lasted only about fifty years after its foundation, it covered hundreds of acres and consisted of beautiful palaces, gardens, artificial lakes, polo grounds, and a race course. Every building was decorated with finely wrought ornamentation of stucco, examples of which have been turned up in the area's excavation. The tower or ziggurat of Samarra still stands, an awe-inspiring monument. After Samarra was abandoned, the caliphs returned to Baghdad, which remained their capital until the fall of the Abbasside dynasty.

Muqtadir was the eighteenth caliph, ruling from A.D. 908 to 936. When he met with the envoy of emperor Constantine VII for the exchange of prisoners of war, he wished to impress him with the wealth and might of his kingdom. He therefore staged, with great pomp and ceremony, a parade along the route to the palace. This road was lined with cavalry, footmen, eunuchs, the caliph's chamberlain, and a number of fierce lions. So impressed was the envoy of the emperor that he was caught by surprise, and mistook first the chamberlain and then the vizier for the caliph himself as he passed through their rooms on the way to the Hall of the Tree where the prince was seated. There, inside the palace, was an artificial tree, adjacent to a huge circular tank of clear water. The tree had eighteen branches, on which sat birds of many varieties made of gold and silver. When the wind blew, the hundreds of delicate leaves moved and the birds sang. Actually the tree was manipulated by an expertly made hidden mechanism.

During this period of the Golden Age, ambassadors were exchanged with many lands, trade and commerce were conducted, and delegates were even sent to China and India to establish trade relations. They returned bearing fabulous gifts as tokens of Eastern good will.

Baghdad was an open market for all merchants and every kind of goods. Like Sinbad, the native traders ventured by sea and land to far-off countries and thus played a large part in Iraq's prosperity. Their ships sailed to China for silk and porcelain, to India for spices, to Zanzibar and East Africa for ivory and gold.

The general prosperity and luxury of this period produced an intellectual awakening, and thus it is looked upon by historians as a time of real significance—not only in the history of Islam but in the development of the world's thought and culture. Mesopotamia in general, and Baghdad in particular, became the forming ground of that intellectual society. The Moslem Arabs possessed a tremendous thirst for knowledge. They were ready to learn, and the rich and flourishing Arabic language became a tool by which they hoped to bring about the eventual unity of all religions, all racial minorities within their boundaries. This language was responsible for what we call the "Arabic civilization," at its height during the rule of the caliphate (637 B.C.–A.D. 1258). This was a great body of knowledge, Arabic in language but not primarily Arabic in origin—rather a composite of Egyptian, Persian, Syrian, Greek, Indian, Christian, Jewish, Moslem, Zoroastrian, pagan, and more.

The caliphs might be considered as the pilots of the intellectual awakening of the Moslems, for they attracted to the court the most distinguished scholars of the time regardless of birth, origin, or religious affiliation. Scientists, philosophers, men of arts and letters well versed in Arabic, Greek, and their own tongue whatever it might be—Syriac, Aramaic, Persian, or Indo-European—all were made welcome. An important factor to the contribution made by these scholars was the invention of paper, introduced from China in the eighth century by al-Mansur. He took advantage of this particular discovery to commission literary and scientific works of the learned men who surrounded him. In their libraries were preserved new texts, new translations of the great earlier Greeks, on philosophy, medicine, mathematics—in fact, concerning all branches of learning.

The numbers we use today, called Arabic, were introduced during this period by the Arabs, as was the decimal system. Heretofore the West had relied upon the clumsy Roman-numeral system. The Arabs developed the first adding machines and the abacus. Algebra is an Arab science, and it was during this time that the Arabs first succeeded in solving third- and fourth-degree quotients, and initiated the system of using letters of the alphabet as algebraic symbols. They also perceived the connection between algebra and geometry, and they produced the first mathematical textbooks, in algebra and arithmetic.

Arab scholars were able to remove astronomy from the realm of speculation and from its connection with astrology, and place it solidly as a science. The ninth-century caliph Mamun encouraged the earliest attempts to determine with accuracy the length of a degree of longitude; this experiment was carried out on the plains around Mosul. Arab scientists built the first observatories, one in Baghdad, the other in Damascus. They also improved the Greek astrolabe, and invented many remarkable and accurate instruments to study the stars and to ascertain and measure the distance between celestial bodies.

They established the first apothecary shops and founded the first school of pharmacy. Medicine developed at this time into a profession, and physicians and pharmacists both submitted to examinations before they were licensed. Hospitals were erected, lectures were held for students, and the first traveling clinics and health centers were organized, reaching even to far-outlying regions. Rhazes, known to Arabs as al-Razi, made an enormous contribution to modern medicine with his pioneer work on smallpox and measles. Perhaps the most famous of all Arab doctors was Avicenna, because of his textbook. This book was known as *The Canon,* and became the standard work of the day, not only throughout the Arab world but Europe and the Orient as well.

Calligraphy and penmanship, approved by the Koran, was considered an art, and calligraphers held positions of far greater prestige than the artists and painters of our day. The dignity and beauty of the quotations from the Koran which we see inscribed on mosques and other buildings bear witness to the status of the art. Craftsmen and artists worked together with the calligraphers to produce the most beautiful effects. They not only carved and painted entire stories on the buildings, but they used the decorative Arabesque art style in the making of objects of daily life, such as carpets, saddles, and the tops of tables.

The caliphate was responsible also for the founding of many educational institutions during this period. The most famous of these was *Bayt-al-Hikma,* the "house of wisdom," and it was a combined library, academy, and translation bureau. Of course the mosques served as centers of adult education, where no entrance fee was required and anyone interested could attend the lecture of his choice. Subjects ranged from religion to poetry and the various languages. The fees of the lecturer, incidentally, were paid for out of the state treasury, and his appointment was conferred by the caliph himself.

Literary groups or circles met in the homes of the well-to-do, or even in the palace itself if the caliph was interested in attending. Free discussion and debate was permitted, and followers of all religions could participate. One of the favorite topics for discussion was the relative merit of Christianity and Islam.

The Arabs had given the Christians full freedom to direct the affairs of their community, their religious institutions, and their schools. During the Abbasside rule, the Catholicus or patriarch-elect of the Christian community in Baghdad received his investiture from the caliph himself; accompanied with great ceremony on his way to the court, he received letters patent from the caliph, and was then presented with expensive robes and gifts. It even happened that the caliph was called upon to settle disputes between Nestorians and Jacobites, two Christian sects, as well as those between Christians and Moslems.

On the other hand the Christians and other non-Moslems, referred to as *dhimmis,* were obliged, in return for this religious freedom and independence, to pay both a poll and a land tax far in excess of those levied on Moslems. During certain periods they suffered various humiliations such as the enforced wearing of special clothing, or the nailing of wooden devil images to the doors of their houses.

The public libraries also served as meeting places for scientific discussions and debates. Bookstores had their own importance, and in Baghdad alone it is believed they numbered around a hundred. They were located then, as now, close to the mosque. These shops, besides being a repository of books for sale, were also meeting places for discussion.

❖ 6 ❖

Decay of the Old Order

WHAT HAPPENED to the might and glory of the caliphs, to their famed capitals, their flourishing cities and towns, their trade with other lands, to the canals and waterways and the verdant farmland, to the plains, the deserts, and the region's numerous inhabitants? What caused the decay and final collapse of what was once a land of greatness? The answers are long and many, the causes various.

The Abbasside caliphate ruled the country from 750 to 1258, when the Mongols terminated it by conquest. This five-hundred-year period was the longest in terms of prosperity the region had ever known. But there were tribulations as well as triumphs. For the empire had been founded among peoples of differing ethnic strains and different religious beliefs, and not one of these groups, singly, could control the others.

There were caliphs during the Golden Age who were able to command with some degree of firmness both the religious and political affairs of the country. These ruled between A.D. 750 and 833, at a time when they were faced with major problems both within and without their boundaries. The war with the Byzantines, religious strife between the many sects, to say nothing of unrest between Jew, Moslem, and Christian, the frequent overflow and flooding of the rivers and waterways in the south and consequent devastation when the waters receded, the epidemics and plagues which reduced the population, the high taxes imposed by the caliph and the ruling class in general to support the harem and large number of slaves, and their generally high standard of living—all were hard to handle while at the same time maintaining law and order. These factors contributed to the country's slow decay, which was not only social and economic but moral as well. Family life was destroyed and there was much enmity among various racial elements of the people— among Arabs, Turks, and Persians. By the beginning of the tenth century the caliph had practically no political status left, but was rather a religious figure with little or no power over the fortunes of the country. Culturally, the effects of the Golden Age had not yet been dissipated, but these were the stresses and strains that eventually brought it to an end.

Some towns in other parts of Mesopotamia enjoyed a certain measure of peace and stability, but they had their troubles also. For example, in Basra to the south a group of slaves from East Africa revolted against the authorities and, killing an entire army regiment, gained control of the city and terrorized its inhabitants.

In the north an Arab chieftain of the Hamdanid family took over the region and declared it independent of the central power. Mosul and the neighboring town of Jazira were the seat of their rule.

In the eastern part of the country, provinces were split into different independent states under petty dynasties which cut themselves off from the central authority in Baghdad. One chief of these powerful states was a Persian, a Moslem of the Shiite sect. In the year 945 he and his rugged army from the mountain area by the shores of the Caspian Sea, known as Buwayhid, swept down from the highlands and occupied Baghdad. This chieftain and those who followed him were not only strong enough to rule Iraq from their capital of Shiraz in Persia, but also called themselves sultans and stamped their names on the coins of the land. These Persian sultans ruled the country with unquestioned authority for a century. The power of the caliphate was completely undermined, and the caliphs became mere puppets in the hands of the conquerors.

Most of the small states were united under these men from the north, and an empire almost equal to that of the earlier caliphs came into being. Once again the city of Baghdad saw many improvements; new, beautiful palaces and mosques were erected, and schools and an imposing hospital staffed by good physicians and heavily endowed. Influenced by the Christian vizier in the city, the conquerors built more churches and hospitals. One even married a Persian princess in the hope of continuing his line. But the gradual dissolution and the crumbling of power continued, for the continual strife between members of the dynasty did not come to an end even when they had a common overlord. Nor did the rivalry end between the Shiite and Sunnite Moslem sects; this religious split is still troublesome to this day.

Again the confusion enabled a foreign leader to take power in the person of Seljuk, a Turkoman from Turkestan in central Asia. He was a convert to Islam. By the eleventh century, Seljuk and his formidable nomadic army threatened all western Asia. They swept through most of Persia, and by 1055 occupied all of Iraq. The Turkomans reduced the small amount of power left the caliph, and forced him to sign a document renouncing all rights to the Abbasside caliphate.

Before the end of the eleventh century almost all of western Asia was united as a Moslem kingdom—under the Turks. Even more important, Asia Minor was overrun, and thus the great Byzantine Empire came to an end and the foundation for what is now modern Turkey was begun.

Unfortunately, this period of relative peace and enlightenment was short-lived, for once more the central authority became weak and the inevitable internecine warfare started up again, this time between Seljuk princes and the Crusaders from Europe, who were now threatening Palestine. This division among his enemies gave a flicker of hope to the caliph al-Nasir, who ruled Iraq from 1180 to 1225. Nasir tried desperately to restore his authority and save the country, and he was greatly encouraged in this attempt by Salah-al-Din, or Saladin, the Moslem hero of the crusades. Saladin, a Moslem Kurd and native of what is now northern Iraq, was interested in seeing the caliphate restored to its ancient power and glory, but he was unsuccessful.

Time had finally run out for the caliphate. A storm of gigantic proportions was brewing in central Asia. Gaining in strength and momentum, this new force was destined to change the course of history. It was centered around the person of Genghis Khan, a leader of nomadic Mongolian or Tartar tribes. Energetic and tireless, Genghis Khan succeeded in welding these tribes into a unified, well-organized, and powerful army. It was A.D. 1227. Riding horses and armed with strange bows and arrows, he and six thousand of his Tartars marched southwest across the border of Persia and down the central plain, adding to his band and to his supplies as he went from lands he plundered. In the course of their advance these Mongolian hordes swept all before them—cities, towns, and villages—demolishing mosques, schools, libraries, and all the treasures of Islamic culture they contained.

Being a pagan and an illiterate, Genghis did not for a moment appreciate or understand the meaning of civilization. Northern Iraq fell, including such cities as Mosul, and Samarra to the south. In the ruins left in the wake of the conqueror, thousands were killed and terror spread throughout the land. Genghis knew no shame. Instead he boasted that he was "a whip sent by God to inflict torture and punishment for their sins." His death in 1227 spared the south of the country, below Baghdad, for a short time. But it was only a breathing spell, for the dismantling of the great empire of the caliphs continued under Genghis's grandson Hulagu. When he took over the leadership he continued to plunder the cities, loot their treasure, and kill the inhabitants. Not even peaceful caravans were spared, for their load was of gold and therefore valuable. All monies were used to pay the engineers and military personnel of the Khan, to rebuild the weapons of war, and to feed the army.

In 1254 the powerful Hulagu marched his men south to conquer the rest of Iraq. He advanced upon Baghdad and isolated it. People in the surrounding towns fled to the capital for safety, but the attacking army was at the walls. The desperate caliph, hoping to save the city, destroyed the bridges, but the Mongol leader built mounds and ditches along the walls to serve as foundations for attack. Matters were worsened by the ravages of recent flooding in the surrounding countryside.

The attack on Baghdad began on January 30, 1258. On this day the caliph, finally realizing the hopelessness of his situation and wishing to negotiate, sent a delegation to Hulagu made up of his vizier and the Nestorian patriarch. Since the Mongol was married to a Christian, the caliph hoped the latter might be persuasive. But the two men were given no opportunity to talk or even to see the enemy leader. The attack began, and lasted six days until a part of the tower in the wall collapsed, enabling the enemy to swarm into the city. The caliph and his entire family were put to death and the caliphate put to an end. It is believed that between seven and eight thousand people were savagely butchered, including the high officials, poets, merchants, scholars, and engineers. Apparently the Christians escaped death upon the request of Hulagu's wife. But their monasteries, along with libraries, mosques, schools, public buildings, were demolished. The burning and plundering continued for a month, and it is said that the Tigris was swollen with waves of blood. Books and other loot thrown into the river made a dam in it, while gold and silver were stacked before the house commandeered by the Mongol leader. Only an unbearable stench from the unburied dead forced him to abandon the city temporarily, leaving it in the command of his officers.

As a result of this holocaust, the economic life of the country collapsed and trade, commerce, and industry were reduced to nothing. The fertile countryside, once a model of agriculture, and the irrigation system of dikes and canals responsible for it that had been maintained since ancient times as a source of wealth and prosperity —all were left in utter ruin. The breakdown of local government was complete, and social disintegration and chaos existed from the north down to the Shatt-al-Arab.

Once-settled areas were reoccupied by Bedouin tribes, and eventually returned to desert or pasture and were used for grazing. The gradual silting and flooding and lack of care of the two rivers and their waterways had the greatest damaging effect upon the country. Iraq has not yet fully recovered from this disaster. Baghdad was no longer "capital beyond compare," the seat of culture and the glory of a Golden Age. It was reduced to the position of chief city in a frontier province, and stripped of its glamour. It became a city of mourning.

By the end of the first half of the thirteenth century the Mongols had control of the largest empire the world has ever seen. It extended from the borders of China and the Oxus River to Central Europe. Even part of Russia was under their rule. Three generations after Hulagu, internal troubles once more brought another dynasty to power. At the beginning of the fifteenth century a further Mongol invasion swept into the country, led by Timur Leng, or Tamerlane, the son of a Turkish chieftain. Tamerlane was powerful and ambitious. In 1393 he attacked Baghdad and massacred thousands of its inhabitants. The "city of peace" was again turned into a field of blood. It is said that Tamerlane boasted of the pyramids of severed heads piled high in the streets. The destruction of the ancient culture begun by Hulagu was thus completed. As in the past, Iraq became once more a battleground between competing powers: the Turks on the one hand and the Persians on the other. In 1509 the country was occupied by a Persian, Shah Ismail, who was a Moslem of the Shiite sect. Naturally this was not pleasing to the rival Turks of Asia Minor or Anatolia, who in the course of two hundred years had expanded from a small clan to prominence and prestige. Once the Ottoman (Turkish) position was secure in Europe, the Turks turned their faces east and south. Thus they came into direct conflict with the Savavid Persians.

In 1534 the Turkish sultan, Suleiman the Magnificent, marched at the head of his well-equipped army down from the north through the mountains of Kurdistan. With no great difficulty or bloodshed, he drove out the Persians occupying Baghdad and returned to Asia Minor and his capital of Constantinople. Suleiman then claimed the title of sultan and caliph.

The Ottoman Turks reorganized the civil government of Iraq to conform to the Turkish pattern. Thus Iraq remained as part of the Ottoman Empire from 1534 until 1918. There was but one interruption, when the country was once again captured by the Persians. Iraq was nothing but a buffer land between the two great Asiatic empires of Turkey and Persia. The center of Islam had, of course, shifted from Baghdad to Constantinople.

But the Turks did not find it easy to govern Iraq. For one thing, it was remote from the central authority. For another, the rule of the pashas was rather ineffective: they were corrupt, autocratic in their administration, caring little for the welfare of the people and uninterested in improving conditions in the country.

Khadimain Mosque.

In spite of isolated improvements, the country at the start of the twentieth century was poor, exhausted economically and socially. Her strength had been sapped even while a vast potential in resources remained untapped. The irrigation system, which was vital to the prosperity of this desert land, had fallen into ruin. Only a miracle could bring the country back to life.

Western European interest in Iraq had existed as early as the seventeenth century, and due to British trade through the Persian Gulf and a French mission to Baghdad, Iraq gradually came to be regarded as important by the West. European interest in the wealth of Asia and India was growing, and a shorter and safer route to Africa was possible through the Suez Canal and the Red Sea. With the diminishing power of the Ottoman Empire, the influence of the Western bloc increased, as all competed for the commercial benefits waiting to be exploited. This received added momentum when in 1907 Turkey granted Germany a concession to build a railway from Berlin to Baghdad. This was later connected with Basra and the gulf.

Real progress toward independence from Turkish rule came when a group of enlightened, highly nationalistic young Iraqi, educated in Turkey and Europe as army officers and inspired by the political activities of the "young Turks," took a long look at the backwardness of their own country compared to Egypt and other lands farther to the west. Some of them even joined Arab nationalist secret societies based in Egypt and Syria. These young men were pledged to get rid of the despotic Turkish rule, which they believed was responsible for the woeful state of their country.

In 1914, when hostilities began between Germany and Britain, the Allies declared war on Turkey, and shortly afterward British and Indian troops landed at Basra to protect the Anglo-Persian oil and safeguard the route to India. By 1915 troops had advanced farther north, to the inland regions and to Baghdad. Meanwhile negotiations were continuing between the Allies and Arab leaders, who agreed to lead a revolt against the Turks, provided that Britain and its allies would recognize the independence of all Arab countries. This revolt broke out on June 5, 1916, and actually made a considerable contribution to the Allied cause. The rebellion was led by the sherif of Mecca and his three sons, members of the Hashimite family and direct descendants of Mohammed. Faisal, one of the sherif's sons, was the key personality of the uprising. Following the organization and the beginnings of the revolt, Faisal and his associates were joined by the Englishman, T. E. Lawrence. Many Iraqi took part in this revolution, and later helped to shape the destiny of their country.

The Arab leaders had gone to war confident that the promises made to them would be fulfilled. They were unaware, however, of a secret agreement which had been made between England and France in May of 1916, known as the Sykes-Picot Agreement. This agreement provided for the division of the conquered territory among the Allies rather than relinquishing it to the Arabs. Still another blow was rendered to the Arab cause when it was learned that the British Foreign Secretary, the Earl of Balfour, had promised leaders of the Zionist movement in November of 1917 that the British people would "view with favor the establishment of a national home for the Jewish people in Palestine" and would "use their best endeavors to facilitate the achievement of this object."

The British victory in Iraq was a foregone conclusion after the capital fell on March 11, 1917. Mosul fell a few days after the armistice was proclaimed in Europe in November of the following year. Thus the country from the north to the Persian Gulf was under British occupation. The war was over.

In January 1918 President Woodrow Wilson had included among his famous fourteen points the provision that nationalities other than Turkish which had been under Turkish rule "Should be assured an . . . unmolested opportunity of autonomous development." From Wilson's words the Arabs took renewed hope.

In 1919 Prince Faisal arrived at the peace conference in Paris, heading a delegation which hoped to obtain fulfillment of Allied pledges. Faisal was at this time the head of the newly formed Arab national government in Syria. For the Arab cause the peace conference was a failure. Then in April, 1920, another conference was held at San Remo in Italy, where the fate of the Arab countries was decided. Instead of the promised independence, it was agreed that the area between the Mediterranean and the Persian border should be divided between France and England; this was decided over the objections of other Western powers who were present, the United States among them. Iraq was assigned to Great Britain under a mandate. When this news reached Iraq, the people felt themselves betrayed. Instead of their promised independence they had received nothing; they had merely exchanged one foreign master for another.

◈ 7 ◈

Revolution and Independence

THE BRITISH MANDATE in Iraq lasted for thirteen years. Referred to by the Arabs as *intidab,* it was denounced by all people generally and by the nationalist leaders in particular. The Iraqi Arabs had joined with the Allies against the Moslem Turks, even though these Allies were foreign to the Arabs in language, race, and religion, on the understanding that Iraq and other Arab lands would be granted full independence. The Arab word for independence is *istiqlal,* and nothing less was acceptable, at least to the nationalists. Hope was high that after six centuries of foreign domination the country would at last be free. In Syria, with Prince Faisal on the throne, an Arab government was already in existence. In Egypt, Arab leaders were vociferous in their demands for self-government. But in Iraq the cry of *istiqlal* went unheard, and growing nationalist feeling was ignored.

After the peace conference the British continued with their own plans for the country's organization and began to implement them. A civilian government was installed under a high commissioner, much on the pattern of the British colonial government of India, and apparently it was intended that Iraq would eventually become a part of the British Indian Empire. Some cooler heads, perhaps more realistic, believed that the mandate was a necessary guarantee against further Ottoman threats or invasion and reoccupation. But the tension mounted. By April of 1920, when the mandate was officially announced, this tension reached its peak. The press had been muzzled, political parties banned, and public gatherings forbidden. In July of 1920 the French occupied Syria and ousted Faisal, who was then left without a throne.

Capitalizing on the universal discontent, the nationalist leaders called on both Moslem sects, the Sunnite and the Shiite, to unite and join with all the people against the British oppressors. Meeting in the mosques for prayer, they delivered political speeches, urging self-government. In the summer of 1920 a holy war was declared.

Revolt broke out first among those tribes who had always resented outside rule, who had been independent even under the Ottomans, and who refused to submit to any authority other than that imposed by their own chiefs. These tribes were in the south and central valley of the Euphrates. Their arms were crude and antiquated, but their faith in Arab destiny was profound. Their neighbors, the Syrians, supported them, and the Shiite holy cities of Kabala and Najaf became centers for nationalist leaders, who sent out a general call to arms.

The uprising spread to Baghdad and surrounding towns, and northward to Mosul. The revolt lasted only a few months, but material loss was high. The British had spent almost a million pounds sterling on the war, and the country itself suffered considerable damage; many of the projects begun by the British were harmed, wiped out, or at least halted temporarily.

In England, public opinion favored the immediate evacuation of troops from Iraq and an end to the occupation. Mindful of this feeling at home, the British established in Iraq a form of national government. This was limited to some extent by the advice and control of the mandate, but it did convey at least a form of statehood. The Iraqi people, feeling at last successful in demonstrating their wish for independence, were triumphant.

That same year the British high commissioner set up a provisional government made up of a council of ministers chosen from among prominent Iraqi and presided over by the chief of the nobles of Baghdad. The men who formed the cabinet at that time belonged to leading families, although not all of Arab blood; some had achieved prominence in service to the sultan, others were merchants, and some were ex-soldiers in the Turkish army. In the meantime a conference on colonial affairs was held in Cairo in 1921, chaired by Winston Churchill of England, who was then Colonial Secretary. Included in subjects under discussion was Iraq's future and it was decided to establish a democratic form of government with Prince Faisal, who had lost Syria to France. Faisal, a hero of the Arab rebellion, was at first reluctant to accept the Iraqi throne, for he was unsure of the peoples' wishes. A national plebiscite was held, therefore, that same year, and Faisal was elected by a tremendous majority. In a great ceremony on August 23, 1921, he was proclaimed king of Iraq. For the first time in six centuries Baghdad resumed her ancient role of state capital.

Faisal was thirty-seven years old when he ascended the throne. He was born in Mecca and had been brought up among the desert Bedouin. A deputy during Ottoman occupation, he fought the Turks, and joined in the Arab revolt of 1916, which was for the purpose of ridding the land of the despotic Turkish rule. Since then he had been looked upon as one of the Arabs' coming leaders.

Faisal clearly realized that his task was a difficult one, but because of his enormous personal appeal he was able to unite the different elements among his people. He had the backing of the nationalists. Religious leaders respected him as well, since his family descended in direct line from the Prophet. And because he spoke their language, the Arabic of the desert, he had the tribal sheiks and their followers solidly behind him.

Faisal was tall and slim, with olive complexion. A small beard added to his dignified appearance. Sometimes he wore Arab clothes and flowing headdress, sometimes a simple khaki uniform or European dress. He was in no way ostentatious, and drove an ordinary car or rode an Arabian horse to get from place to place. Baghdad had not kept up the palaces of the caliphs, and Faisal lived in the citadel situated in the north gate not far from the banks of the Tigris. This citadel had been used as a residence by the governors or pashas under the Ottomans. Around the king were the officers with whom he had fought in the days of the revolt. Among them were Jafar Askari, Jamil Madfa'i, Nuri al Said, and others. We must remember Nuri, for he was to play a prominent role in shaping the destiny of Iraq for almost forty years. The British writer Gertrude Bell was a great admirer of the king; she had traveled widely in the Middle East, and her books are unique. Because of her deep interest in and knowledge of the countries, she had served as Oriental secretary and adviser to the High Commissioner in Baghdad. And as she was deeply interested in archaeology, she founded the Baghdad Museum.

In 1922 Iraq and Great Britain drafted and signed a treaty that set 1932 as the year for the termination of the mandate and the independence of Iraq. Agreement was reached on financial, military, and judicial assistance on Britain's part. An assembly was established for the purpose of drafting a constitution to initiate a government, by electorial law, that was democratic and modeled after the British constitutional monarchy. There were to be two chambers, one appointed by the king with its authority carried out by a cabinet, and the other elected by the people. Unfortunately, the British who were helping draft this constitution did not take into consideration the fact that there were not enough people in Iraq capable of serving in parliament or holding high government posts. Only a small number had had sufficient training to fill civil-service jobs, and most of these were Christians who had studied in church schools. It was natural, then, that there were Christian ministers holding cabinet office. The first Minister of Finance was Sasun Haskil, a Jew. Unhappily, the vast majority of the people, who were Moslems, at this time were illiterate. Conditioned to century after century of despotic rule, they lacked all experience in any sort of self-government or its procedures.

Nevertheless, much had been achieved in the years between the setting up of the kingdom and independence. One of the first matters to be dealt with was the fixing of international boundaries. Since Turkish claims to Mosul had not been settled, the League of Nations

named a Commission of Inquiry; as a result of this body's delibera-
tions, the city was granted to Iraq in 1925. The boundaries between
Iraq and its neighbors Turkey, Syria, Saudi Arabia, and Persia were
also more clearly defined. A further step forward in Iraq's progress
as an independent nation came on October 3, 1932, when she was
admitted to the League of Nations as an independent sovereign state.
This, of course, added greatly to the stature of the king.

Between the years 1921 and 1932 the population had increased,
the standard of living had risen, and the civil administration was
adequately staffed with British-trained civil servants. Good courts
were operating, and new schools, colleges, hospitals and clinics were
set up. For the first time in centuries a nucleus of an army and police
force existed who were capable of carrying out their duties. A new
Iraqi currency was put into circulation to replace the Indian money
of the mandate. Exploration for oil had already begun, and this
greatest of the country's national resources was at last being exploited. Revenues began trickling into the national purse and a new
outlook permeated the minds of administrators, who began plans for
modern city streets, electricity and running water, for roads connecting cities and towns with outlying rural areas, for new railroads between cities and linking Iraq with her neighbors. Steamboats began
operating up and down the rivers, carrying passengers and commercial traffic to ports on the gulf.

A new era had begun also for the 100,000 Christians in Iraq, as
well as the Jews and other minorities. Under the new government
peace and order were assured, and greater tranquillity and security
existed than the people had known for many years. Monks, priests,
and bishops were afforded protection by the government, which did
not interfere in any way in the affairs of churches or monasteries,
synagogues or other places of worship.

King Faisal, at the head of the kingdom during this most difficult
period, played a large role in the creation of the new state and in the
shaping of its destiny. His burden was heavy, his problems too many
and too complex. Illness resulted. It was reported that he began
spending his sleepness nights strolling alone along the banks of the

Tigris. He would converse with the boatmen waiting for customers alongside their *balams*. He listened to their stories of their experiences, to their problems, and he tried to help them. Sometimes he would recite a poem to them. They did not know who he was, but he became a familiar figure along the moonlit banks of the river. Finally he was forced to go to Switzerland for medical treatment, and died there in September 1933. The entire population mourned him. Faisal was buried in the mausoleum, but his belongings and relics can be seen in a small Baghdad museum.

Ghazi, Faisal's twenty-year-old son, succeeded him. But his reign was full of unrest, as political and religious dissatisfactions caused the fall of one cabinet after another. The young king Ghazi was killed in an automobile accident, and his infant son Faisal II succeeded him. Prince Abdul Ilah served as regent to his infant nephew.

When World War II erupted, relations between Iraq and Britain cooled further and were finally severed. In 1940 a shift in political attitudes and the general rise of nationalist feeling once more brought Iraq into direct conflict with her allies, England especially, over the interpretation of a treaty regarding passage of British troops over Iraqi soil. Because of their opposition to anti-British sentiment, the boy king, the regent, and all cabinet members were forced to leave the country. The British landed their troops and refused recognition to the new government. Open war was the result, and the consequent British bombardment took several civilian lives. But hoped-for German help did not come and Iraq was forced to sign an armistice with Britain. The king and his entourage returned. Many of those who had participated in the action against the British were put on trial and some were even condemned to death. Hundreds of people thought to be pro-German were interned, and this included all merchants who had dealt with the enemy. Some were even hanged in the public square. There was press censorship, and once again the British were firmly in command. There is little doubt that this occupation of Iraq was of great importance to Great Britain, for the country not only served as a military base, but also war materiel could be shipped from Basra through Persia to Russia. During this occupation the country prospered, revenues continued to increase, and jobs were plentiful. Morale was high.

After the war Iraq joined the United Nations as a founding member and also the Arab League, playing host to many Arab nationalists. By sending troops, she also participated in the Arab-Israeli conflict that broke out in the spring of 1948. This was caused by the voting in the UN on the partition of Palestine. Like all Arab countries today, Iraq is technically at war with Israel, since no peace treaty has ever been signed. Actually this is one of the few issues on which all Arab lands agree; for the most part they are divided by their political differences.

Discontent was smoldering beneath the surface, for World War II had not brought the expected freedom. Everyone was disheartened by the defeat in Palestine and the consequent influx of close to one million refugees into adjacent Arab lands. The Arabs, whose people had also lived in Palestine for hundreds of years, felt strongly that it was as much their land as the Jews'. They held the British and the United States both responsible for the creation of the state of Israel. The youth of Iraq, just graduated from college, were frustrated that they were able to participate so little in their country's affairs and believed that the government and the regent at its head were far too pro-West. The young king, Faisal II, they said, was dominated by his uncle, the regent, and was far too weak to be relied upon to stand on his own feet.

Trouble, bound to occur sooner or later, came when news of the Anglo-Iraqi treaty revision reached Iraq in January of 1948. Opposition was so great that demonstrations and rioting broke out. Many among the students and opposing police were killed, and the army was forced to step in to restore order. The government fell and, as a result, the treaty just revised was repudiated. The new cabinet formed by Nuri al Said declared martial law. Nuri was a powerful politician who had assumed leadership many times since Iraq's independence, and he succeeded after World War II in achieving for his country a measure of political stability.

King Faisal II came of age on August 2, 1953, when he was sixteen. A great celebration took place, and the jubilation was shared by the entire country.

It was during the premiership of Dr. Fadil Jamali that the idea of the Baghdad Pact was born; it was to be an alliance of Middle Eastern countries, to operate, like NATO, against threats of Soviet aggression. Fadil was a graduate of Columbia University in New York. Married to an American, he represented his country at the United Nations, where he spoke up frequently for the Arab cause. His opponents, however, felt him to be too pro-West, and in 1954 the king called once again on Nuri to form a cabinet. But in spite of the apparent stability of this new government, discontent was open. The prime minister was concerned over communist infiltration, and not only revised the Anglo-Iraq treaty but began to put the Baghdad Pact into operation. The countries involved in this alliance were Turkey, Iran, Pakistan, Great Britain, and Iraq. While the United States was not a member, she supported the pact by offering military and economic aid when necessary. All diplomatic relations ended between Iraq and the Soviet Union.

But the people of Iraq, the nationalists in particular, were strongly against any treaty that bound their country to England or Turkey, their enemies of long standing, or to any foreign power for that matter. Past experience had made them distrustful; they vastly preferred a closer relationship with neighboring Arab countries.

Premier Nuri al Said took precautions against any possible opposition coups. He dissolved all political parties, put hundreds of nationalists—most of them students—in jail, and imposed a strict censorship on the press. He also took personal safeguards, for there were many rumors of attacks on his life. It was under these dubious conditions, with loud opposition by Egypt and Syria heard offstage, that the Baghdad Treaty was signed.

For the next few years the Arab world was in ferment. The joint attack in 1956 on Egypt's Suez Canal by England and France, with some help from Israel, naturally caused an explosion in an already smoldering situation. There were riots and demonstrations in Baghdad, Mosul, Najaf, and other cities. Demands made for the severing of diplomatic relations with Britain and France actually forced a rupture with the latter. And the figure of Gamal Abdul Nasser of Egypt was emerging as one on whom people could pin hopes of Arab unity.

The betrothal of the young king Faisal II to a Turkish princess in 1957 was highly unpopular. It seemed obvious that this was for the purpose of bringing Iraq and Turkey closer together. The nationalists, of course, had hoped Faisal would marry an Arab girl from one of the neighboring countries.

In February 1958 the union of Syria and Egypt into what was called the United Arab Republic was officially announced, followed by a federation between Iraq and Jordan. The rulers of these two countries, Faisal and Hussein, were cousins, and both belonged to the Hashemite family. Again it was Nuri who was called on to form a cabinet at this time to make sure the union was not one in name only.

In the summer of the same year 6,000 American marines landed in Lebanon at that government's request, following a political crisis caused by a United Arab Republic threat attracting worldwide attention. Iraq, led by Nuri, was the first among the Arab states to offer assistance to the pro-West Lebanese president. A meeting of Baghdad Pact countries was scheduled for July 14 in Istanbul, and Faisal and Nuri planned to leave Iraq together to attend the meeting in Turkey. From there Faisal intended to journey to England to meet his fiancée.

During the early morning hours of July 14, 1958, when people still slept on their cool rooftops, a group of army officers marched to the capital, led by Brigadier General Abdel Karim Kassem and accompanied by army units stationed in Baghdad. The coup resulted in the taking over of the country. The young king was murdered, as were many of the royal family and household.

When the people woke on the morning of July 14, they heard over their radios that the monarchy and the old regime had fallen. The formation of a republic with Kassem at the helm was proclaimed. Crowds gathered in the public squares and there were demonstrations of joy. In spite of the fact that there was some disruption of public services, rejoicing was general and celebrations appeared in order.

Two days after the *coup d'état* Nuri al Said was captured and killed while trying to leave the country in disguise. The monarchy came to an end; the constitution was annulled and a provisional constitution proclaimed. On July 27 the withdrawal from the Baghdad Pact was announced.

What were the causes of the revolution? In part it was the great general dislike many of the people had for Nuri; the crown prince was also hated by many. It was these two men who had shaped the country's political destiny for many years. It was considered that both were tools of British imperialistic ambition, and that the governments over which they presided were practically police states. In truth their power had been absolute; parliament had governed in name only, elections had been fixed, and all opposition suppressed by jailing its leaders. Freedom of speech and the press did not exist. There was obvious corruption in the administration. Prices were high, the standard of living low, and the educated young people of the middle classes were given little opportunity to take part in their country's government. The young Arab nationalists cried that the old regime had failed utterly to put any reform into effect; they believed that feudalism and imperialist thinking hindered the country's progress. The Palestine war, with its consequent stream of Arab refugees, proved another constant source of discontent. As for the Baghdad Pact, it had been unpopular from the start, and any alliances with Turkey, blamed for decades of despotic rule, were held as betrayals.

What these young Iraqi wanted was a closer relationship with other Arab nations. When England and France, with help from Israel, invaded Egypt, the indignation of the people could not be suppressed. Hatred of the West was universal, and Nasser became the symbol of Arab nationalism.

Kassem, however, was unable to fulfill the people's hopes for better government. Within months after his regime took over, there was a struggle for power and ideology between the incumbent

Ba'ath party and one which was disposed toward the United Arab Republic. Revolts took place in Mosul and in Kirkuk, and there was a Kurdish uprising in the north. Economic conditions worsened, the country was isolated from its neighbors, and foreign investments were curtailed because of the government's instability. As a result, the country was wide open to communist influence from Russia. On February 8, 1963, another revolution took place and the pro-communist Kassem government was overthrown by the Iraqi Army. Kassem was killed, and the second Republic was formed. Later in the same year the government was taken over by Marshall Abdel Salam Aref, Kassem's former supporter. Aref's aim, however was not a restoration of Kassem's policies, but the establishment of a socialist government friendly to Egypt's President Nasser.

⊗ 8 ⊗

Baghdad

BAGHDAD, the Paris and Rome of the medieval world—heir to Ur, Babylon, Nineveh, and Ctesiphon and home of the fabulous caliphs of the past—is today the capital of modern Iraq. Here are the seat of government, the country's financial center, the hub of commerce, communications, the press, and radio, television, and entertainment, and here is the largest concentration of the country's industries. Over a million people live in this city where the old and the new meet and merge.

The Tigris River divides Baghdad into two sections. The eastern section is referred to as the Rasafa. This constitutes the major part of the city where the majority of the population lives, where government buildings are located, as well as the business establishments, shops, movie houses, hotels, restaurants and modern clubs.

The western section is the Karkh. Here are the airport, the railroad station, and a new government building which was started by the previous administration. Here are also the new Iraqi museum, the television and radio stations, up-to-date residential houses and a new housing development, a country club with golf course, swimming pool, and tennis courts.

Today the face of modern Baghdad reflects the country's pride of progress: modern hotels have risen along the banks of the historic river, and the city's skyline of modern banks, office buildings, and business establishments resembles in many ways an American or Western city. The new structures rise over the quiet old mosques and the busy bazaars. Baghdad also shares with other modern cities parking problems and a high toll of traffic accidents. It is a noisy city, more so even than New York, for when a jam of cars makes drivers impatient, blowing horns from all directions is not an offense or against any regulation.

Baghdad has many daily newspapers and weekly periodicals, an Iraq news agency, a broadcasting station, and a television station—

Al-Rashid Street, twentieth century Baghdad.

the first in the Arab countries. There are also a few learned societies and research institutions, public as well as private libraries, and a number of museums. Great interest is shown by the people in art exhibits where the young Iraqi artists exhibit and sell their work.

In greater Baghdad the larger industrial enterprises are electricity and water supply, brick and cement manufacturing, small-unit industry concerned with food and drink processing, date packing, breweries, cigarette making, spinning and weaving, chemicals, furniture, shoemaking and jewelry. There is an oil refinery not far from Baghdad that is run by the government.

Although modern Baghdad lacks the beauty of the ancient city, there is a ring to her name that spells magic the world over. To young and old this is the city of Aladdin, of Sinbad, and of Kismet; it is a land where dreams are born. To scholars it is a place filled with antiquity, where a corner is turned and a centuries-old monument is glimpsed, a museum filled with tablets or jewelry of long ago, or a dusty bookshop where examples of elegant Arabic calligraphy are piled from floor to ceiling. To the writer—like Agatha Christie perhaps, who actually wrote some of her mystery stories here—it is a city of adventure. To the reporter it is a capital where the unexpected happens every hour on the hour. And to the tourist Baghdad is a fascinating place where an ambitious and forward-moving young republic can be studied against the background of its country's history.

The laying of the city's foundation stone by the caliph al-Mansur in A.D. 762 was preceded by many months of planning and deliberation. He chose for this monument to his rule a site a little to the north of Baghdad West, on the banks of the Tigris.

Mansur's capital was a masterpiece of design, and it was arranged cleverly in many ways. For example, the caliph was able to leave the city unseen by all save his personal guards. In addition, any disturbance within the city walls could be dealt with easily. Not only the palace, but the living quarters of high officials and even government offices were out of reach of the ordinary townspeople.

Today, however, Baghdad is much like other modern cities, accessible by all methods of travel to the entire country and to other parts of the world. By whatever route the visitor chooses to enter the city, he will go through attractive suburbs, with parks and beautiful villas set in well-lighted paved streets that lead to the center of Baghdad. But should you as a tourist hope to take back with you snapshots to remind you of the city's history, you would be doomed to disappointment. Little remains from the romantic past outside of the museums, except for the bazaars, which were built in the Middle Ages.

Bridge in modern Baghdad.

Rashid Street, the main thoroughfare, is about thirteen miles long, and cuts through Baghdad from north to south. It is a modern city street, along which pass Fords, Chevrolets, Volkswagens, and even English double-decker buses. New-looking office buildings rise from the ground. There are neon signs, and window displays very much like those seen in Western cities, showing refrigerators, TV sets, or shavers. On the sidewalk a businessman or woman shopper hurries

Colonnaded Al-Rashid Street in Baghdad.

by in European dress; but there will also be the bearded Arab of the desert in his flowing robe, a colorfully clad Kurd from the north, or even, though rare today, a long-gowned woman with a veil. On this commercial city street there is not much that is unfamiliar, apart from the babel of strange tongues and the odd lettering on signs and posters. To find what is unusual about Baghdad, we must strike away from the modern streets to the back alleyways, towards *Shari' al Nahr,* "the street of the river." Here, instead of stores or office buildings, there are the little shops of the silversmiths, operated by the sabaeans, or Mandaeans, who claim John the Baptist as their teacher and who believe that the flowing river is the symbol of the saint's life.

The shops—almost stalls really—are none of them more than a dozen feet wide and barely twenty-four deep, and inside them sit barefoot old men with beards who, in their short white robes, look like the prophets pictured in the Bible. A young apprentice divides his time between tending the tiny charcoal brazier and learning the silversmith's art from his employer. Most of these artisans can neither read nor write, but with just three or four tools are able to fashion the most intricate and delicate work, in black or in colors and of all shapes and sizes, from a tea set to jewelry. They are remarkable craftsmen, and are proud of the skill displayed in their work, a skill handed down from father to son.

Leaving the silver shops, we come to Bank Street, where are, as the name implies, the banking establishments of Baghdad. It is one of the city's busiest streets, where financial speculations and many kinds of business deals are conducted, as in any other large city. But set in between the stately banks on both sides of the old walled street are coffeehouses, usually crowded with men who sit sipping the thick Turkish brew or the unsweetened Arabic coffee. On the street itself porters go up and down, clad in quilted jackets and carrying great bundles on their stooped backs. They bend low, balancing the heavy load with the help of a head strap, and they call out as they pass, *"balak, balak,"* which means "watch out, watch out."

As we stand on Rashid Street, we look down one of the side streets and see low couches against the walls—bright splotches of color, for they are covered with Persian rugs. Sitting on them are the rug sellers, with their gleaming white or green turbans. If we take this street away from the main thoroughfare, we can make our way through the archway to a covered bazaar. Here, on twisting, narrow alleys, are half-lit shops and little windowless stalls where much of the commerce that is carried on has little relation to modern goods. But even here where the past is so evident we may expect to see modern European dress side by side with the veil and the aba.

We come first to shops where silk and wool cloth are sold by the yard. It comes from all over the world. A little farther on are rug shops, with rolled carpets stacked from floor to ceiling—Persians, gay and colorful hand-woven rugs, pressed-wool, quilts, and sheepskins, all of them typical of individual towns and villages in Iraq and nearby countries. A little below the level of the street are shops where we can buy clothing of all kinds—trousers and jackets or hand-woven camel's-hair aba; and here, perhaps to keep them in, are tin boxes and chests decorated with carvings or studded with brass nails. The variety to be found in the bazaar community of Baghdad is fascinating and endless. There are slipper makers, and leather shops where the saddle and harness makers work. Farther on are the bookshops that remind us for all the world of the days of the Abbasside period and the glory of the caliphs, for here we can see the ornate and flowing penmanship of the Arabic calligraphy. Books and manuscripts are stacked to the ceiling, and every inch of floor space is covered with them too.

Returning to the more modern part of the city near the government buildings and the post office, we see a man sitting at a table on the sidewalk, sheltered from the glare of the sun by a red or green umbrella. He is the scribe. In this man, who is a letter writer by profession, is embodied one of the country's most important institutions, though perhaps the smallest.

Not far from the post office is the copper market, the *Suq al Safafir*. It is on a street so narrow, two donkeys cannot pass each other. Each coppersmith works in a shop that seems like a small, dark cave, in the center of which burns a fire. The proprietor of the shop stands to one side, shaping his bowls, ash trays, pots, pans, and candlesticks over the flame, hammering and fashioning the beautiful objects that are sought after by tourist and resident alike.

The *Suq al-Atatir* is the bazaar where the perfume shops are to be found, and its name has been the same since the days of the caliphs. Near by are the little booths and stalls where many sorts of herbs and aromatic spices are sold.

In another street there is one of the loveliest and most unusual

Copper market in Baghdad.

Arcaded bazaars overflow with goods and people.

sections to be found in all of Baghdad, for here are the shops selling beads. They glitter in the half-lit bazaar, their variety of form
excelled only by their many colors: purple, blue, amber, pink—some
delicate in shade, others brilliant; some threaded with silver, some
with gold. Looking at these beads, we realize that practically all the
Iraqi who are not in Western dress wear them. Today, as in the past,
these beads constitute the jewelry worn by women and children in
cities, towns, villages, desert—in fact, all over the country. Even men

carry them, for a beautiful and expensive string of amber, known as a *masbaha*, is a source of pride to an Iraqi; it is told like a rosary in spare time, or is worn and used as a sort of pacifier or as an occupier of the hands to cut down on smoking.

In these back streets of the city the bazaars are endless. There are shops where stacks of pottery and water jars of all sizes line the floors. Some of them, dipped in a deep-blue glaze, remind one of the oil jars in the tale of Ali Baba and the forty thieves. In the high sheen of his ware are reflected the pale face and dark beard of the potter. His shop is busy, for pottery, as in former times, is used in every household, rich and poor alike.

Right here would be a good place to begin a tour of the city's mosques, for the Marjan, or coral mosque, is in this bazaar; most men working in the neighborhood take time to perform their noon prayers in it. The mosque was built in the fourteenth century by Marjan ibn Abdullah, who rose from poverty to become governor of Baghdad; its beautiful gateway and the exquisite minaret and dome form one of the city's landmarks. Adjoining it was once a madrasa, or school, a two-story building around an open court, with cells and rooms for the students, its walls decorated with flowing Arabic inscriptions. There was a library attached to the mosque.

The famous minaret of *Suq al Ghazil*, the "bazaar of the yarn," only a few hundred yards away, is all that remains of the mosque attached to the palace of the Abbasside caliphs that was built in the ninth century A.D.

Not far away, but in a northerly direction, is part of the palace of Mamun, built also during the Abbasside. It is richly decorated, with ornamented bricks inside the cupolas. Today the palace is a museum of Islamic art.

Back where we began our tour of the bazaars, near the street called Shari' al Nahr, which runs alongside the river Tigris, was one of the great Baghdad colleges known as the Mustansiryah. Built in A.D. 1234 and named after its founder, the caliph Mustansir, it was meant originally as a seminary for the study of Islamic religion and law, and contained a magnificent library. Once one of the city's

Mustansiriyah University. This Arab university was founded in Baghdad 1234 A.D.

finest buildings, the two-storied façade can still be seen from the river, and the Arabic inscriptions on its walls can be deciphered on closer inspection. But nothing remains of the kitchen, baths, storage room for the cooling of water, the famous brick vaulting, the entrance clock, or the lamps for the oil to light the students at their work. It is said that the college cost 700,000 dinars to build, and possessed an endowment of a million dinars. But it is hoped that the government's Department of Antiquities will be able to restore some of its former glory, for the building is considered a national monument.

Crossing the main bridge to the west side of the city, we come to an interesting group of tombs and shrines, once the cemetery of the caliphate. The first we see is said to be the tomb of the lady Zubayda, the favorite wife of Harun al-Rashid. The tomb is of a curious pineapple-shaped construction, with a spire made up of a series of arches. Inside there are row on row of connecting cells, whose walls and ceilings are pierced with round holes through which stream the rays of the sun to light the interior in crisscrossed beams of gold.

About four miles to the north of Baghdad is the glorious mosque of the Kadhimain, a landmark to travelers entering the city from the west. Under the blazing noonday sun, or even at dawn or in the dimness of twilight, the gold of the two great domes and four lofty minarets gleams unforgettably. One must approach this mosque on foot, going through the narrow, winding streets of the little town of Kadhim, which sprang up around it. Only Moslems may enter the picturesque gateways which are aglow with pink and blue tiles. Inside are gardens filled with many-colored flowers, and a huge court-yard in which stands the mosque itself. Today thousands of Shiite Moslems visit this shrine every year, coming from remote sections of Iraq, Persia, and Asia. Many bring their dead so that their bodies may lie on this sacred soil.

We have talked before about the ruins of Ctesiphon, twenty miles to the south of the city on the left bank of the Tigris, and we remember that this was the winter capital of the Parthian Persians when their power was at its height and when they governed practically the entire Near East. It is here that the country's most striking ruins are to be found. Built in part, it is conjectured, after 130 B.C. by the Parthian Persian kings and added to in the sixth century A.D. by the Persians and the Sassanians who followed them, this was a magnificent royal palace. Little remains today of this triumph of architecture and engineering. Only the main reception hall and one wing of the palace façade still stand, but it is worth seeing, for the vaulted roof is the largest span of unreinforced brickwork to be found in the world. Today these ruins stand on desolate desert sands, inhabited only by the storks who nest among the broken bricks.

It is mostly in Baghdad's museums that we can look at the rich store of art and artifacts from the country's past. The Iraq Museum especially tells us about the people who lived here from many thousands of years before Christ until 637 years after his death. Items from four periods of civilization are exhibited. Soon the contents of this priceless storehouse will be moved to a new building designed by the late American architect Frank Lloyd Wright.

Unlike many modern cities, Baghdad has not grown upward toward the sky, but rather has spread out from the center of town, up and down the river and out around the suburbs. Its length is close to fourteen times its breadth. It is still the old part of the city, Haydar Khana, which remains the busiest, with narrow, winding streets barely wide enough for two horsemen to pass, let alone two automobiles. The houses here are not more than two stories in height, built around an open court, with their overhanging wooden roofs almost touching the roofs of the houses on the opposite side of the street. There are no sidewalks, and the outer walls of the houses rise directly from the street itself, giving greater privacy and protection. This style of architecture has been used all over the country for hundreds of years and is probably even much like the style of Abraham's house when he lived in Ur before his migration to Palestine.

The new section, Karrada, provides a striking contrast, with broad, tree-lined boulevards, islanded in the center and planted with flowers and shrubs. The residential streets are paved and well lighted. There are housing developments and there are villas with their own date groves or private gardens; it is here the well-to-do and middle class of the city live, whether they are Moslems, Christians, or Jews. Some of the houses were designed by architects educated in the West, or at least greatly influenced by the West. But all have the customary flat roof with the parapet that shields the owner from his neighbor's prying eyes. On these roofs, as Iraqi have done through the centuries, the people dine and sleep during the hottest months when the temperature may get as high as 115°. The hottest part of the day is spent down in the *serdab*, or cellar, sunk below the level of the first floor. In spite of the air conditioning used in most of these modern homes, the old and tried methods still prevail; one of the oldest ways still used to cool the house is to cover the windows with thatched shutters, kept dripping wet.

The chief building material is brick, made from the Iraqi clay that has always been in use in the center and south of the country. Of course cement, asbestos, concrete blocks, and slabs of marble brought down from the north supplement the usual sun-baked brick.

Because of the great influx to the capital from cities, towns, and villages all over the country, the population of Baghdad has soared to over a million. Many people work for the government. Unskilled laborers work in the cement, brick, textile, soap, and cigarette factories, in the oil refineries, in the industrial plants mushrooming all over the area. Actually most of the country's industries are concentrated in and around the capital. And hundreds of students come to study at the university's many branches. After the 1954 flood there were thousands of refugees from the southern marshlands, who came with families, buffaloes, and belongings to settle down in the *sarifa,* or outskirts, or on the vacant lots between villas. The government has been making an effort to establish these people in permanent homes and eliminate the slum conditions that their arrival caused.

Because Baghdad is the seat of the government of Iraq, representatives of all the diverse elements that make up the population of the country can be seen here. It is also the center of the communications system, and has the greatest number of newspapers. Here, too, are many museums, an art center, and an academy of music, and soon there will be an opera house. It is a modern capital, with all that this implies. What makes it different from other capitals in Western eyes is the strangely exotic glimpses it offers of other cultures.

In December of 1962 a dual festival took place, commemorating the 1000th anniversary of the founding of this famed city and paying homage to its noted philosopher al-Kindi, who died 1,000 years ago. Today Baghdad is once again on the way toward reclaiming its former prominent role in world civilization.

◈ 9 ◈

Mosul

WE WILL MAKE several stops of interest on our way to Mosul, the second-largest city in the country. Striking north from Baghdad, we come first to Samarra, about seventy miles to the northwest of the capital. This is one of the most fascinating cities of Iraq, as it is built within the confines of the ancient city on the same site. Near by are the remains of a Christian monastery dating from sometime before Samarra became the capital of the Abbasside dynasty (between A.D. 836 and 876). The outstanding monument remaining from the Golden Age of the caliphs is the Malwiyah or spiral minaret of the great Friday Mosque, one of the oldest in the country. The structure, copied from the ziggurat of Babylon, has a wide, winding ramp on the outside of the minaret. Although the mosque has vanished, the tower of the minaret remains one of the greatest structures of the Middle East.

Samarra is not important as a secular city today, but it does rank as a great religious center with many shrines and mosques. In the modern town there is a particularly lovely mosque that rises out of the narrow, winding streets, its dome of beaten gold gleaming in the sun; delicate Persian tiles decorate the minaret. This is the shrine of the tomb of al-Mahidi, who, the Moslems believe, will one day return to earth and announce the triumph of Islam over the whole

The ziggurat, or circular minaret, of the Friday Mosque of Samarra.

world. Then a universal reign of peace and equality will prevail among all men.

Leaving Samarra behind us, we drive onward to the eastern side of the Tigris. The scene changes completely here from the flat, desolate central plains to the rolling, undulating land of the north. Building materials are no longer the mud and brick that we are familiar with in the south, but stone and alabaster. Groves of date palm have been replaced by orchards of olive, and by wild oak. We no longer see Arabs only, in their flowing robes and abas, but also the strong, picturesquely clad Kurds from the hills around Kirkuk, Erbil, and Mosul. In the background rise the majestic snow-capped mountains of Kurdistan, looking south onto what was once the mighty Assyrian Empire. We are reminded of the archaeologists' discoveries when we catch sight of the grassy mounds covering ancient ruins scattered among fields of wheat and grain; even five thousand years before Christ people tilled here, and harvested, and gained their sustenance from the land. But by and large in this part of Iraq the many, many years of a farming culture are forgotten because of the excitement generated by the discovery of the liquid wealth flowing underneath the soil.

The center of this great reservoir of oil is the town of Kirkuk, which during the Ottoman Empire was part of the *villayat,* or province, of Mosul. At the end of the First World War the question of whose jurisdiction Mosul would fall under was a knotty one. After many months of discussion the League of Nations granted control of Mosul to Iraq, with a concession of its oil yield granted to the British, Dutch, French and American interests in 1926 so that the rich deposits could be exploited to the full. The controlling organization was known as the Iraq Petroleum Company, based in Kirkuk. Because of the income from its oil, Iraq at last had a sound economic foundation on which to build its future, and programs for the improvement of the country and people could be developed and implemented.

As we approach Kirkuk, the first thing we see are huge jets of flame shooting up into the air. These are from the refineries. But out of the ground come smaller flames, caused by natural gas escaping from the wells to relieve the underground pressure. They are a reddish yellow and burn day and night. For centuries they have burned upward from cracks in the ground, rekindling themselves if extinguished by man or nature. Through the years shepherds and mountain people have often used their heat for warmth or for cooking. Now this natural gas is being tapped.

Not far away are the rigs and storage tanks of the great reservoirs. The petroleum company has constructed three large pipes, the largest measuring 30 inches in diameter, across the Syrian desert to carry the crude oil a distance of some 550 miles to tankers lying offshore in the Mediterranean. The smaller pipes terminate in Tripoli, Lebanon, and in Syria. By means of the oil these pipes carry, the spark of

An oil rig in modern Iraq.

new life has come back to the city of Kirkuk, founded as far back as 3000 B.C. Marco Polo, passing through the town around A.D. 1294 on the way to the Far East, gave it the name of Circura, which changed over the years to Kirkuk. Because the steady influx of workers to the oil fields has tripled the city's population over the last twenty-five years, Kirkuk is now the fourth-largest city in Iraq. Many of these men are highly skilled. The oil company operates its own schools, in addition to those in the community run by the government, and has its own hospitals and clinics for the benefit of the workers and their families. This place is now a modern city, with parks, paved streets, churches and mosques.

Sixty-five miles north of Kirkuk is Erbil, or Arbela as the Greeks knew it; before them it was called The City of the Four Gods by the Assyrians. This city is thought to be one of the oldest in the world. Its surrounding flatlands witnessed the fighting of many battles, among them the titanic struggle between Alexander the Great and Darius III of Persia in 331 B.C. Darius' treasures, it is believed, lie buried far beneath today's cellars. This community has been continuously inhabited since its first settlement. City lies atop city, each succeeding one built over the ruins of the past. And because it was designated as a holy city, still thickly inhabited, no excavation was permitted. It is chiefly because of its fine water supply that Erbil survived through the ages, for there was no need for its inhabitants to move away in search of more water. One of the magnificent monuments probably buried beneath the huge mound or tell that is the modern city is the famous temple of Ishtar, who was the great mother goddess of the Assyrians, and whom the mighty kings came to consult before they embarked on a new campaign of pillage and destruction.

Through the centuries traders, nomads, and merchants with their caravans of goods passed through the region. And today also it is a trading center, lying, like Mosul, Kirkuk, and Sulaimaniya, on the paved road that joins the north. A railroad system connects the city to Baghdad and other centers of commerce to the south.

Forty-five miles northwest of Erbil, on the other side of the Great Zab River, tributary of the Tigris, we come to Mosul, on the banks

Leaning minaret of the Great Mosque at Mosul, built in 1172 A.D. by the Atabegs. The tilt was carefully designed by the architect.

of the Tigris itself. This city, second-largest in Iraq and boasting 180,000 inhabitants, is sometimes referred to as *Hadba,* or Hunchback, because of its suggestive silhouette seen against the skyline as one approaches from Nineveh. It is a beautiful city, rising high above the waters of the river and set in fertile fields of wheat. The region is in general agricultural, and after the rains the soil looks dark, rich, and fruitful.

The slopes and valleys of the plains extending for miles around the city are carpeted with all sorts of flowers, especially in the springtime.

Mosul, often called "The City of the Two Springs," was once known principally for the fine and delicate fabric known as muslin. This material not only brought fame and trade to Mosul, but added a word to the English language. Actually, little or no muslin is made in Mosul today, but the people are rightly proud of the other textiles they do produce.

On the plains and highlands and in the valleys around Mosul are scattered many villages. Although they are only a few miles apart, each of these little communities has its own language, beliefs, method of worship, its own customs, habits, shrines, traditions, and a way of dressing that is peculiarly its own. Many of these traditions take us back to the early days of civilization. In Mosul lives not only the Mutassarif, or governor, of the province, but many dignitaries of the various creeds and churches as well. There are one hundred mosques in Mosul and many, many ancient churches and shrines. The main body of the population is Arab, but there are also Assyrians (Nestorians), Turkomans, and others.

As is usual in this northern part of Iraq, the houses are built mostly of unhewn stone cemented together with mortar and plastered over with mud. In the better houses as well as in the modern villas hewn stones, marble, and slabs of beautiful alabaster are used for construction. These slabs are also to be found in the paving of floors and sidewalks, and all come from quarries close to the city. The high cost of timber makes it difficult to get wood for building purposes, except for doors and window sills.

The streets of the city are long, winding, narrow lanes, scarcely wide enough for cars to pass each other. There are two main streets that are wider, and these cross each other so that the city is divided into four quadrants. Like all Iraq cities of any size, Mosul has many bazaars. Stalls crowd together at the edges of narrow, cobbled streets; shoppers, clothed in the many traditional costumes of their native village, jostle and push, and those who sell also buy in their turn the rice, tea, coffee or cloth to be found in the stalls. The few women seen in the bazaars wear the black aba, or loose gown, that completely covers the face and body. They have come from the surrounding villages and are selling eggs or yogurt on round wooden trays, or perhaps they are offering cream in small clay dishes. In the more modern parts of the city women for the most part do not cover their faces, and the younger people everywhere are beginning to discard this ancient custom. Indoor bazaars, some of them around an open court, are vaulted and have tiny windows high up that let in the light like the shafts of an arrow. Coffeehouses abound, and in them men sit on the mat-covered wooden benches, sipping coffee and sometimes actually conducting business over coffee as a Western man might over luncheon.

A bridge connects the two sides of the city. Today it is made of steel, for the ancient pontoon bridge that was more picturesque had to be replaced. On the bridge the meeting of the old and the new is especially dramatic, for we can see a modern car trying to pass by an ox-drawn cart, a string of camels, and some donkeys laden with

The bridge at Mosul a hundred years ago, as seen by a contemporary artist.

black tents, pots, pans, and chickens. The impatient occupant of the car waits while members of the caravan argue back and forth, shoving their sheep and goats and their frightened dogs out of the way. Shepherds and drivers all shout and struggle in the crush as they cross and meet on the bridge. Along the riverbank below, women washing clothes are beating them with pieces of wood as they stretch out the clothes on smooth slabs of marble or stone. When clean, these clothes are spread out on the grass or pebbles to dry, and it is a lovely sight to see them gleaming in the sunlight, spread out against the green of the bank. Usually a boy sits near by to guard them from a grasping, soiling hand or wayward wind.

On the side of the bridge farthest from town the ground is stony, full of pebbles. Here there is a souk, the farmers' market, that operates only in late spring and summer and fall, when there is produce to sell. The men and women from neighboring villages, all colorfully clad, gather during the earliest hours of the morning and are finished with their business by the time the sun rises; thus they avoid the heat of the day.

Goods are peddled on a wholesale basis, as people of the city buy things for their houses, restaurants, or to sell in shops. Exchanged in the noisy bartering that goes on are vegetables, watermelons, tomatoes, lambs, goats, donkeys, bundles of camel skins and bales of wool.

About a mile east of Mosul, only yards from the huge tell that marks the city of Nineveh, is the shrine of Nebi Yunus, he that was Jonah of the Bible. All religious sects consider this to be a great shrine; a mosque with a graceful minaret beside it crowns the top of a tiny hill near by. Beneath the soil of this hill lies the palace of an Assyrian king.

According to tradition, Jonah was sent by God to preach to the sinful people of Nineveh, but was swallowed up by a whale. For three days and nights he cowered in its belly, until he was cast up unharmed somewhere on the Syrian shore. From there he made his way to Mesopotamia. The floor of Jonah's shrine is paved with lovely blue and green tiles, and the story is that the prophet's body lies buried beneath it. The tomb itself is covered over with a green veil, and Persian carpets soften the floor with bright color. Pilgrims of all faiths visit the shrine to pay homage or pray to Jonah.

The city of Mosul today, however, contains little that explains its title of "queen of the cities." The importance of Mosul as a center of trade diminished greatly over the years, but the city is again taking its rightful place because of the vast mineral resources in the earth that are finally being exploited. The city is also a center for the surrounding agricultural district. There are textile, sugar, and cement factories that provide employment for the city's workers.

Mountains to the north form a natural barrier between Iraq and neighboring Turkey and Iran. These mountains rise generally about 3,500 feet, with peaks that tower as high as 11,000 feet, and the fine views and cool, healthful air make the region a resort spot for city vacationers. The region is also becoming popular as a winter-sports center. New hotels, rest homes, and guest houses are being built, with swimming pools and other modern attractions, and the government is contributing large sums for the promotion of the area. This is possible because a good road, a railway, and an air route link Mosul with Baghdad and other cities to the south.

The schools and colleges are good in Mosul, and there is a medical school and a library and a fine museum housing treasures found in the mounds around the city.

◈ 10 ◈

Basra

BASRA, one of the least-known of the cities of the Middle East, is actually one of the most colorful and picturesque. Third-largest city in the country, with a population of some 200,000 inhabitants, it lies close to the confluence of the Tigris and the Euphrates, which unite at Qurna about forty miles to the north. There they form the Shatt-al-Arab, which, joined by the Karun, another great river and the longest river in neighboring Iran, flows down to the Persian Gulf.

About 270 miles to the southeast of Baghdad, Basra is joined to the capital by rail and air, and of course by the waterway of the Tigris. The vast floodlands surrounding the city make the land immensely fertile, and the dates grown in the region around the Basra have for this reason long been known as the largest and best in the world.

The city was founded in 638 by the caliph Omar and was then, as now, strategically located on the trade routes using the Persian Gulf. In the early days of the Moslem conquest Basra was a military base and a recruiting center for the army. Later, during the Abbasside caliphate, the city was highly prized, since it was the very gateway to Arabia. Fifty years after it was founded it had a population of 300,000 (larger by 100,000 than it has today) and had risen in this comparatively short period to a position of power and wealth. The city enjoyed considerable prestige as a cultural center, particularly in the reign of Harun al-Rashid.

Basra was famous in literature as the city Bassorah, and was the scene of many of Sinbad's fantastic adventures. Today the actual port of Basra is at Margil, the city itself being about two miles inland from the river. This section of Basra, known as the old city, contains a network of canals most of which connect with the river. The third part of the city is known as Ashar, an international community made up of residences and commercial establishments.

There is an amusing story about Nearchus, an admiral of the fleet of Alexander the Great, who navigated the Shatt-al-Arab on his way to Babylon. He sailed from the mouth of the Indus along the south coast of Asia to the Euphrates. But at the spot near Basra where the Tigris joined the Euphrates, a sandstorm is said to have caused him to enter the Tigris instead of the Euphrates, as he intended. He and his entire fleet sailed for days confidently up the wrong river.

For hundreds of years Basra was the scene of military activity. As the Abbasside caliphate declined, so did the position of Basra as a cultural center. But it still remained strategically important, and for many decades the Turks and the Persians fought over it.

The Turks were in possession of the city from 1668 until the early months of World War I. On November 23, 1914, as a result of a battle lost to British forces, the Turks finally were driven out of the region. The city and surrounding countryside became a British supply and military base, and the center of operations for the Anglo-Persian Oil Company. For the duration of the war Basra remained a British enclave, but at its end the city was included in the newly created kingdom of Iraq.

During the period of their occupancy, the British modernized the port by constructing new wharves and docking facilities, by building warehouses and installing electricity and steam cranes for loading and unloading ships. They also initiated extensive dredging operations in the river channels, so that large ships could enter the port.

The development of the oil industry in the Persian Gulf did much to stimulate the rapid resurgence of the city of Basra, but it did not acquire its present status as a great port until World War II, when cargo ships from the British Empire and the United States brought millions of tons of war material, food, and medicines to the city for shipment overland to the Soviet Union.

The Basra Oil Company tankers carried oil to European ports; exports of barley and wheat left Basra, and the port became the world's first in the export of dates. Today, besides being the water gateway to Iraq, it is the southern terminus of the Iraq railways, part of a system reaching all the way to Europe. Basra is also a center for airlines flying from Europe to the Far East. The newly exploited oil field at Zubayr, ten miles inland, and the huge storage tanks at the mouth of the gulf make Basra of prime importance. One third of Iraq's oil is exported through this port.

Going north from Fao, an oil-tanker terminus near the mouth of the Shatt-al-Arab, a motor highway follows the river that divides the Persian and Arab worlds—the Persian Aryans on the east side and the Arab Semites on the west. Both banks of the river are lined for miles with groves of date palm. Probably no river in the world carries such a variety of water traffic, for on it one sees ocean liners of great size that dwarf the smaller craft like cabin cruisers, fishing boats, yachts, and dhows. The dhow, often with gaily colored or patchwork sail, is the counterpart of the sailing vessel of biblical days, and probably much like that on which Sinbad set out for his voyage of discovery.

A little more than forty miles upsteam from Basra toward Baghdad is Qurna, at the juncture of the rivers. Here, in the delta land to the east, is the Tigris, while to the west one sees the Euphrates. The once-muddy rivers now run swift and clear, having lost most of their silt in the swamps.

The marshlands of the delta region shelter a way of life unchanged for centuries. Here the Ma'dan, whom we described earlier, live as their Sumerian ancestors did five thousand years before. These marshlands cover an area about a hundred miles long and thirty to forty miles across. The small, thin-grained rice grown in this region is highly prized, very nutritious, and considered by many to be the world's finest.

Few cities in the Middle East have the peculiar charm of Basra. It has been called the Venice of the East, and with reason, for canals actually take the place of streets and highways in many parts of the city. These waterways serve row on row of balconied houses built directly on the banks of the river. Some of the canals have been in existence for hundreds of years. The people of Basra, rich or poor, now as in the past, literally live on the water. Their lives revolve around water—the river, the canals, or the great fertilization and irrigation ditches of the miles and miles of date palms.

In the central part of the city ancient styles of architecture, wearing apparel, and transportation merge easily into today's life, which revolves around ultramodern buildings, Western-style dresses, and rapid transit. In the midst of groves of aged date palms we find magnificent modern homes set in colorful tropical gardens and velvet lawns.

The social and economic forces of the city are complex. Hundreds of nomadic and seminomadic peoples live in primitive conditions not much better than those of their Ma'dan neighbors, while the new, Westernized merchant class live under the most modern conditions. In the narrow, roofed streets of the old city—the bazaar or shopping center—are displayed baskets made of date fronds, beds made from tree trunks, or strange fish from the waters of the Shatt-al-Arab or the gulf. But one also finds silks from China and India, textiles from Damascus, Milan, and Birmingham, nylon and other synthetics from the United States, and gadgets of every description from Japan, as well as silverware of rare beauty from Amara in Iraq, colorful rugs from Persia, and robes of every kind of material from the far corners of the Orient.

The people of Basra, like Iraqis in general, are partial to outdoor life, whether in the countryside outside of the city or on and near the water. Basra and its environs, with hundreds of square miles of date groves and endless waterways, offer many diversions for the picnicker or lover of boats.

In Basra no one is ever far from the date plantations and their network of irrigation canals. Since the tides in the gulf affect the water level of the Shatt-al-Arab, the date canals and creeks are supplied with fresh water daily, as the tide rises and causes the river to back up and flood to just about the right level of the carefully engineered waterways. Other canals in the city profit also from this inundation. Basra is unquestionably the date capital of the world. More than three fourths of the world's dates are grown here. Rich alluvial soil and unlimited water for irrigation, the long growing season, moderate rainfall and abundant sunshine all contribute to making Basra's dates the finest there are.

The ancients referred to the date palm as the "eternal tree of life" and in southern Iraq trade in this fruit has an ancient history. The

Dates, man's oldest and most nutritious food, are shipped at Basrah to the four corners of the earth.

Date harvest in Iraq.

Koran, holy book of the Moslem religion, refers to the date thus: "Honor the palm tree, for it is thy father's sister, and it has been given the name of the blessed tree because it was created from the remainder of the clay of which Adam was made."

The date as food for local consumption and as a luxury item for export is, along with oil, at the very foundation of Basra and Iraq economy. Some 300,000 tons are grown annually in Iraq, bringing an income of 16 million dollars. In our Western world we eat dates as dessert or as candy, but in Iraq and other Eastern countries it is an important part of the daily diet for thousands of people, the nomads of the desert and countryside especially.

The Basra date industry, housed today in modern plants and packing houses, employs thousands of men and women from the city and surrounding villages. Many hands are needed in the journey from tree to shop. When the dates are harvested they are carried to the plants, where they are washed, graded, fumigated against parasites and mold. After packing in many forms of bulk and package sizes, the fruit is sold for domestic and export markets. Fancy dates are stuffed with walnuts or almonds and put up in attractive wooden-and-cellophane packages to be sent to all parts of the world.

Basra boasts a modern mechanical packing plant and a chemical fertilizer factory. A paper mill and a TV station are under construction, and one of the largest grain silos in the Middle East nears completion on the Shatt-al-Arab.

Basra today enjoys a unique position among the cities of Iraq. It is the country's one outlet for ocean-going commerce, and the greater exploitation of oil resources has raised the port to one of world importance. Employment—in oil, dates, shipping, exports and imports—is high. Basra is an ancient city, where a leisurely water-borne way of life exists side by side with the drive, frenzy, and motivation of modern commerce in a progressive new metropolis.

❖ 11 ❖

Holy Days, Feast Days, and Social Institutions

THE PEOPLE of Iraq, whether they live in the city, in a country village, or deep in the desert, and whatever their economic circumstances, love to slough off their daily responsibilities and problems to celebrate the many feast days and holy days of their land. This is particularly true in the rural areas and smaller towns or villages. There the everyday routine is so ordered, and the social life so limited, that an event such as a birth, baptism, circumcision, betrothal, marriage or even a death is treated as an important and exciting ceremony. Actually the religious festivities connected with such events constitute the chief recreational outlet for Iraqi people of all ages, and this holds true even in the urban parts of the country. One can imagine the number of such celebrations when one considers the diverse religious and ethnic make-up of the people, all living in close contact, yet each with a separate existence, very individual traditions and way of dressing, and often speaking a completely different language.

Great enthusiasm is shown all over Iraq for parades, demonstrations of army power, sports events, and speeches by the President or other highly placed government officials. There are several rather general holidays. Because Iraq is predominantly a Moslem country Friday is the official day of rest, instead of Sunday as in Christian countries, and it is on Fridays that the government offices, banks,

125

Iraqi men playing chess.

and most places of business are closed. No law, however, decrees that shops and other establishments must close on these days, and apart from government employees, everyone, whether Moslem, Christian, Jew or whatever, is free to work or not.

One of the most important facets of the Moslem religion is the observance of Ramadan, the ninth month of the Moslem lunar year. Ramadan, which comes in cycle during every season of the year, marks the period in which the Koran was revealed to Mohammed, and the approximately 500 million Moslems in the world all observe it. This month is designated as a month of fasting, when nothing is taken into the body from before sunrise until after sunset. The Koran says: "Eat and drink until so much of the dawn appears that a white thread may be distinguished from a black, then keep the fast completely until night."

Moslems are supposed to refrain from sinful thoughts or deeds during Ramadan, and—possibly to make this easier—all radio and television programs are canceled. No places of amusement are visited by the true believer. Only the news and the weather are broadcast, and religious programs, which include the reading of the Koran and the voice of the muezzin calling on the faithful to pray. It is the custom at this time of the year for the President to pardon certain prisoners whose terms have but a short time left to run.

At the end of this holy month there begins a tremendous holiday called Id al-Fitr, the "breaking of the fast." It lasts for three days and is celebrated by Moslems all over Iraq. Among the well-to-do in the cities it is spent mostly at home. The head of the house stays in, to welcome friends coming to wish him a happy holiday—*Ayyamakum Saida.* His wife, although she may be unveiled, nevertheless keeps out of sight when she is not making sure the visitors receive their share of sweetmeats, pastries, and thick Turkish coffee. Usually the family gathers for a big meal in the evening, but the elders might go instead to a dance at a country club or social hall. During the days of feasting the children visit with their relatives or promenade up and down the main street, gazing in at shop windows that are especially lavish in their displays of candies. They wear their best clothes, and are usually given a small sum of money to spend as they choose.

Less wealthy and sophisticated Iraqi men pass the days of the feast in their favorite coffeehouse. These centers are really social institutions in Iraq, and in them club meetings and other gatherings are held. Turkish coffee or tea is served from a giant samovar which is kept continually boiling and, if it is summertime, Western-style cola drinks are often seen. Eating a snack of liver broiled with onion over charcoal, the men watch television or listen to the radio or to the storyteller or newspaper reader, who entertains those unable to read for themselves. Perhaps, while they sit drawing on the hubble-bubble (a long, coiled, water-cooled pipe), they listen to the village chief, or to the sheik of the tribe if they live in the desert.

In more rural parts of the country, the days of feasting occupy a still more prominent part in the life of the community. For most it is one of the rare occasions when new clothes and shoes are bought from money saved for that purpose all year long. Nearly everywhere in Iraq, except in the cities, shoes are a luxury, worn only on special occasions.

The girls, brilliantly clothed, stroll in groups around the village square or sit in a doorway, showing off their new finery. Boys will accompany their fathers to the house of the *mukhtar,* or village chief, or go with friends to spend holiday pennies on sugar candy or inexpensive toys from the village store. Women gossip for a while before starting the lengthy process of preparing the meal, which, on this special day, often means the killing of a lamb.

For the Christians in Iraq, as for Christians everywhere, one of the two most celebrated holidays of the year is Christmas. In Iraq it is strictly a religious holiday. During three days of celebration, all shops or businesses operated by Christians are closed, and Christians visit their friends and relatives to whom they wish *Idkum Mubarek,* Happy Christmas, and with whom they share a glass of liqueur or coffee. Few are the houses where a Christmas tree is found; certainly there are none outside of Baghdad. Just as the Moslems mark their holy day, all members of the Christian family will have new clothes if it is possible, and the children will be given money to spend.

The housewife rarely leaves her house during the several days' celebration, as she must spend many hours beforehand preparing the traditional food, so she will not have to cook on Christmas Day itself. *Yachni* is the customary dish; it consists of the meat of at least half a lamb, and requires lengthy preparation. Finished as a rule on Christmas Eve or early Christmas morning, this dish is often served for breakfast following Mass, or for lunch to the gathering relatives.

The Mass, attended by all adults, takes place shortly before dawn, for it is believed that it was at this hour Jesus was born. After a family breakfast, the children are dressed in their new clothes and sent out to spend their money. In cities or villages, boys go out together if they are not with their fathers. Each house in the town or village parish is visited in turn by the bishop, his priests, and his colorfully dressed *kawwas,* or attendant, and the occupants receive a blessing.

Easter is celebrated with possibly even greater fervor than Christmas in Iraq. In large cities the three days of celebration are marked by churchgoing, the visiting of friends, and many family gatherings over the traditional dish called *zibibiya.* Basically this is the same as the Christmas food, but raisins and figs are included. Pastries, preserves, and date cookies are traditional for all holidays.

Because the majority of Christians live in Mosul and surrounding villages, Easter is celebrated there in the north more elaborately than elsewhere. Spring is at its best in this part of Iraq, and families from far away journey to the region and stay several days, visiting the different monasteries and shrines that dot the countryside. Every village has its costumes and traditional dances.

For the most part Christians and Moslems live together in harmony throughout Iraq. They go to school together, work together in business or trade; both can serve in the Moslem government, and both share a common patriotism in peace and in crisis. And while the Christians do make up the bulk of visitors to the north during Eastertime, citizens of all faiths, without regard to their beliefs, visit the shrines and monasteries of long ago. Many take their sick and troubled to a church where a saint lies buried, sometimes spending many nights in prayer near the grave. Many drink the medicinal water from the holy springs, and the more religious carry back to their homes some dust or earth from the holy places they have seen. Another custom of the devout is to leave a piece of their clothing tied to a tree near the site of a martyr's death.

It is in the springtime, when the surrounding plains are blanketed with flowers, that most people visit these shrines of the north. They may go for the day, or stay perhaps for the whole season in rooms rented for their family. Some summer resorts have been set up near holy places, and those in the cool mountain regions are particularly popular. The Iraqi make these journeys with great faith, spending days and nights in prayer. Many believe that a particular saint will come to them and heal their illness or help with their spiritual problems. Many come away from these retreats convinced that they have been visited by the saint and that a miracle of healing or spiritual rehabilitation has taken place. It might be said that the monasteries and shrines of Iraq are the psychoanalytical clinics of the East.

The most memorable of the spring festivals held near Mosul is that of the Yezidis. It is known as *tawwafa,* or "pilgrimage to the shrines," and marks the new year for this strange religion. It comes sometime between the third week in April and the first week in May. While there are many Yezidi festivals or celebrations taking place simultaneously in a few of the northern villages, the most popular ones occur in two neighboring villages some ten miles to the northeast of Mosul. These lie close to natural springs at the foot of a mountain, and the wild flowers to be seen in nearby valleys and the plain provide a carpet of riotous color for these ancient rites.

On the night before the feast each family kills a lamb, taking the meat to be put on the holy graves and, later, to be given to the poor. From there the men and women and children proceed to the meadow where the ceremony is held. All are dressed colorfully—the women especially, with kerchief-swathed heads, many necklaces of colored beads, and wide, bright sashes. The musicians, playing on pipe and drum, stand in the center, while around them begins the traditional dance known as the *debka.* Linking arms, the dancers swing round and round in an uneven circle, shifting their weight from one foot to the other while the Emir, their prince and religious leader, walks about nodding his approval. Usually there is a crowd of onlookers made up of Christians, Moslems, Jews and members of other sects, mostly from the cities. Enthusiastic but orderly, the spectators join in the clapping and in the *tahlil,* a cry set up by the women during the height of the excitement. No police protection is necessary. These rites have been taking place for hundreds of years without interruption save in time of war or famine. It is usual for food to be spread out on the grass of the surrounding field and anybody is welcome to share in it. No alcohol is served but there is no prohibition against it among the Yezidis.

A visit to the shrines interrupts the three days of celebration, and there certain rites and ceremonies are performed. No one who is not a member of the sect is allowed there, for it is a religion whose secrets are not revealed to outsiders.

The gayest and most exciting of secular holidays in Iraq are the weddings. There are many, of course, in all communities, and they are elaborate, with interesting accompanying rites that vary from one village to another and from one sect to another. The origins of many of these ceremonies are ancient. While the Western style of weddings has been adopted by the educated class in the big cities, in smaller towns, villages, and the desert the traditional customs still prevail. Festivities last for several days, and the guests are entertained with music and dancing, as well as with wrestling and other athletic spectacles.

In the village there is no one, be he ever so poor, who is not willing to spend his savings for these occasions that give meaning and dignity to his life. These festivities provide the only times that a peasant family can really enjoy a full-sized meal together and allow themselves time away from their daily toil. It is for this reason, to make the occasion most enjoyable, that marriages take place as a rule during the autumn and winter months, for they are less busy.

Marriage between members of two families is pondered over for a long time, because in Iraq marriage does not concern only the prospective bride and groom, or even just the two immediate families. It is of importance to parents, brothers and sisters, and all the many relatives. Actually, the whole village or tribe takes part in the celebration, which usually begins a week before the wedding and continues for a week after the ceremony. Friends come at any time during the feast, perhaps staying for the night to partake of the gaiety. Music is very much a part of it all, and often professional dancers are employed to entertain the guests, depending upon the circumstances of the hosts, who wish to demonstrate their hospitality to all.

Another great event in the life of the family, whether Moslem or Christian—or any other religion, for that matter—is the birth of a child. This is particularly the case if it is the first-born boy, for it is he who will carry on the name of the family, who will bring prestige to the parents and fill them with pride. Everyone will address them as *"abu Ahmad,"* the father of Ahmad, and *"umm Ahmad,"* the mother of Ahmad. Not nearly as much is made of the birth of a girl, for she will marry and become a member of another family; besides, it is held that the cost and trouble of bringing up a girl is far greater to the parents than the upbringing of a boy, with much less to show for it. There is a proverb which says: "A dead father lives through his sons," and this is the philosophy of the Arab. It is of course not as strong a belief among the educated classes living in the cities.

When a boy is born, his relatives watch over him night and day, surrounding him with all kinds of charms to safeguard him against the evil eye. These superstitious practices take many forms: the Kurds, for example, lay a large needle, a knife, or piece of an onion beside the crib. Others place a blue stone and a doll's eye on his clothing. Certain visitors are discouraged, especially women who have not borne children, or those with blue eyes. Should someone who might harm the child approach him, the word *mashalla,* or "God's will is always used," is spoken to ward off any possible hurt.

Three days following the birth of a child there is open house for family and friends, who bring gifts of gold, silver, or clothing. Guests are served refreshments of sweets and coffee, and members of the household give to the poor at this time to express their own gratitude, the amount depending on their wealth and social standing.

In a Moslem family the mullah, who is like a priest, officiates in the naming ceremonies of the child; this takes place seven days after his birth. Among the numerous Christian minorities of Iraq, this naming ceremony is a baptism. The religious rites are simple, and almost identical in city and village; they take place as a rule some forty days after birth, on a Sunday following Mass. A big dinner follows for relatives and friends, and all of them convey their hopes to the parents that they will be present at the wedding of their offspring, and that he will grow in health.

While not so usual in the larger cities, elaborate ceremonies attending the Islamic rites of circumcision are still customary in towns and villages throughout Iraq. This takes place when the boy is around twelve. The ceremonies can last for as long as a week, and there is music, dancing, and entertainment. In this Moslem ceremony the men and women are separated and the entertainers perform for both groups. Frequently some poorer boys of the same age are invited to participate, with their expenses paid and new clothes provided.

There is an unusual and rather lovely ceremony that is part of the Mass celebrated by Iraqi Christians, and it is referred to as *qublat al-salam,* "the kiss of peace." This phrase is spoken every day by the priest at the end of the Mass. He then touches the hands of the two altar boys and they run down the steps of the altar toward the congregation. All the worshiping men, women, and children stretch out their hands toward them, hoping to be touched by the hands of the altar boys and receive a blessing. The priest, meanwhile, prays that this ceremony will bring peace in reality to the hearts of men, as it was brought to the world nearly 2,000 years ago.

An important accomplishment in the life of a Moslem child is the reading of the Koran without any mistake, or the memorizing of a large portion of it. This is known as *al' Khatma,* and entitles the youth or girl to the honorable title of *hafiz,* or "he who memorizes the Koran." It usually takes a year or two of hard work, for this classical book of the Arabs is not easily mastered. When it is done, therefore, the parents celebrate, particularly in small towns and villages where opportunity for getting an education is small, and the achievement therefore greater.

The occasion is usually celebrated, for a boy, by a luncheon, to which the mullah who instructed him and his classmates and relatives are invited. All dress in a *dishdasha* or *zebrun,* colorful traditional clothing. On his head the boy wears a fez decorated with trinkets or dangling charms. The other boys, black skullcaps on their heads, will have their finger tips dipped in henna dye.

On Friday, the Moslem holy day, the boy will occupy the place of honor at the head of a procession, sitting in an *arabana* (carriage), or in an automobile, or perhaps astride a horse or donkey. With him or behind him are his brothers or close relatives. All around are musicians playing the drum, the tambourine, or flute, and chanting verses from the Koran. The parade winds through the streets while onlookers stand in reverence and respect along the wayside. Children who have not been invited sometimes join in, and frequently by the time the procession is over there will be three or four times as many in it as there were at the beginning.

For girls, however, the celebration of this feat of learning takes place at home, with only women present. The girl is dressed in her best clothes and many relatives and friends are invited. Music is supplied by a group of *mulaya,* one of whom instructed the girl. Dressed in black, they beat lightly on the darbukka, a kind of pottery drum, or on the tambourine, and they chant from the Koran. The climax arrives when the girl sits on a little stool set on a stage at the center of the open court where the guests are assembled. In front of her is a walnut stand, inlaid with mother-of-pearl, and on it rests the sacred volume of the Book. Spreading a white cotton scarf on her head and covering all her hair, she opens the Koran and begins to read. The guests are quiet. When she finishes, petals of fresh flowers and rose water are sprinkled over her head, the musicians strike up, the congratulations begin. The girl is surrounded by everyone, showering her with gifts and coins thrown around her little stage. Whatever money there is, is usually given to the musicians. The ceremony is concluded with the serving of a dinner in the open court to all who are present.

For centuries in this part of the world the public baths have been one of the main features in all the cities and larger towns, and they constitute an important social institution in Iraq. Even in the days of the caliphate and the Arabian Nights, the baths were used not merely for ceremonial bathing but also as places of amusement and luxury. According to the accounts of Arab historians, the number of public baths during medieval times, all of them supplied with hot and cold running water, numbered ten thousand.

Today, of course, every modern city house has its own private bathroom. But there is at least one public bath in every section of every city and town throughout the country. Over the centuries these baths have remained a place for relaxation and entertainment, particularly for the women, who otherwise lead a rather limited social life. But the baths do serve men as well. Children are taken by their mothers after they are forty days old. Boys over two years of age accompany their fathers. Nights are reserved, some for women, some for men, and the family can bathe together at least once every two or three weeks. These baths are more or less clubs, where women can entertain, meet friends, gossip, and show off their latest clothes. Rates vary according to the time of day, but are reasonable. A bride is brought to the bath before her wedding day, and the occasion is full of excitement for friends and relatives, as music, dancing, and refreshments are provided. Families hire a bath attendant on a yearly basis; she welcomes all celebrations, whether for births, baptisms, coming of age, or weddings, for it is at this time that she receives the gifts that make up her wages. Her duties include the carrying of clothing and towels between house and bath, the reserving of the booth, and the shampooing of hair.

These public baths figure also in stories told the children of Iraq. Some of these tell of magic-working genii who live in the baths, and others of demons, hideous monsters of a horrible nature who change in shape and size at will and who appear only at night, with some evil scheme ready to carry out. These tales can be found in much Arabic literature as well as in *The Thousand and One Nights.*

⬦ 12 ⬦

Family Life

As IN ALL parts of the Middle East, the family in Iraq is the core around which society revolves. In spite of the strong forces from outside that might have destroyed it, this pattern of life, with its roots and traditions, imposes social and economic controls that have persisted through the centuries. This way of life, built around family solidarity, holds true wherever the family lives, whether in a tent or mansion, a mud hut, villa, or house of reeds. While education and industrialization has, to a degree, extended its influence in the cities and towns, among the desert nomads and in rural communities the pattern of life has changed little since biblical times.

The Bedouin, for example, follows the ancient patriarchal system in which the interests of family, clan, and tribe come first. These are his kin, and here lies his security against the harsh life of the desert. Leadership—that is, government—is provided by the sheik, the leader of the tribe. Support in time of need, trouble, or danger comes from the other members of the tribe.

As we have seen during our visit to the desert, life for the Bedouin is hard, and only the truly strong survive. Mortality is high. Since prestige comes from the number of children, boys in particular, that a family has, children are somewhat indulged and made much of. The young children are taught obedience and respect and are reared strictly according to tribal traditions. Up to the age of four or five, boys and girls play together in the home. When they reach six or seven they are given tasks to fulfill, but still play and live together as brothers and sisters. At eleven or twelve, however, there is a separation of the sexes. Girls are barred from male society, from friendships outside the immediate family circle. A boy at this age accompanies his father in his daily routine; he may tend the sheep, help load and unload when a new pasturage is sought, and go with the father in the evening to the *Mijlis,* a social meeting held in the tent of the sheik in winter and outdoors in summer. All male members of the tribe will be there, sitting in a circle or leaning against the saddle of a camel in the warmth of the fire. The boy sits not beside his father, but unobtrusively in the shadows, trying to catch the talk of raids, of chances for rain or new grazing, or listening to the sheik as he settles disputes.

In the desert, women generally enjoy more freedom than their sisters in the towns and villages. Veils are not worn, but a girl usually wears a black-cotton scarf over her head. A young girl is watched carefully. Her day is spent helping her mother wait on the males of the family, in cooking, kneading bread, or fetching water from well or spring. She learns how to make the daily supply of leban, the yogurt that is such a staple of Middle East diet. She will collect wood for the fire, and spin wool or goat's hair for clothes or tentmaking. Gossip against a Bedouin girl's honor brings disgrace to the family, and her father, husband, or brother is entitled to kill her to regain his own honor. He is protected against punishment for this deed by tribal law, and he will not be brought to justice. Girls usually marry at fifteen or sixteen, while boys wait until they are twenty; it is usually by arrangement. A dowry accompanies the girl when she marries, and can be in the form of cattle, camels, or money. Polygamy is common among Bedouin, as it is among the marsh Arabs to the south. It is not unusual for a sheik to have several wives, even as many as three or four (Moslem law sets a maximum of four wives at one time), and his several families may live close together and take care of each other's children.

In the rural regions of Iraq, family life is very similar to that of the desert, with the family at the center of everything. Family responsibility rests in the hands of the oldest male, who is master of the household. His word is law, even if he is old and unable to work. Under his roof are gathered all the married sons and their descendants to the third generation; all bring him their earnings. As long as his father lives, a young man has no property of his own; everything he has is turned over to his father for the benefit of the family.

In winter all live together in one long, dark room, each son and family together with the parents. Somehow there is little difficulty in controlling so many people, perhaps because respect for age is inherent in the traditions and culture of the country, and children are brought up to adhere to these patterns of society. Intermarriage within the community is important, therefore, for the harmony of the family, and it can be understood that marriage with a stranger is frowned upon. In practical terms, it would be hard to fit a stranger into this very close-knit way of life.

As is the case in many parts of our world, the mother of a family exerts considerable influence, not only on her immediate household, but on society in general; this influence, however, is indirect and subtle. This is especially true of the northern Kurds, who treat their mothers with great respect and consideration, and also, though to a lesser degree, of the marsh Arabs. Christian women in rural societies hold a stronger position than Moslem women in the same community. Divorce is almost unheard of and when it does occur is very one-sided in favor of men.

The frequent absence of men from home throws many duties on the women. But because few women in the rural desert areas ever go into the outside world, their lives are narrow, and they know of little that does not occur close to their doorstep. Besides her domestic chores—the cooking and care of the children and other household needs—the woman must frequently engage in outdoor work such as helping the men in the fields, tending the flocks, weeding the garden, and bringing in the harvest. She will go to market to sell the produce from her land, eggs, yogurt, butter, and vegetables. In her leisure time, such as it is, she will gather around the well with other village women, sit beside the communal oven, or gossip as she spins clothing or knots rugs from the wool of her sheep. It is to the old women of each village that the family turns for advice and consultation.

Children in rural families are brought up much like those in the desert. They are separated in their early teens, the girl to learn the ways of the home, and the boy to accompany his father and be drawn into the world of men. No special entertainment exists for these young people; in the evening they sit with their elders, listening to stories of their experiences. In this way there is developed an intimacy between the children and the grandparents and other elders in the family which grows through the years.

Courtship and flirtation are strictly forbidden, but the youth meet at the well, in the fields, or during feast days. There is no abrupt change that confronts a child as he moves from adolescence to manhood, as happens so often in Western culture. The word "teen-age" does not exist in rural Iraq. The pattern of life starts early, and adulthood is merely an extension of early experiences, rather than readjustment.

Day begins with the dawn in the village, and it ends at sundown when the call to evening prayer is heard. The family gathers for the evening meal, but the father eats with his sons and other male members, while the wife and other women eat what is left. Of an evening the men gather in the coffeehouses to talk or to play trictrac. As they meet in the dusty street they salute each other: *"Al-salamu alaykum,"* or "Peace be with you," and they are answered, *"Wa alaykum as salam."*

Marriage is looked upon differently by those of differing beliefs. To the Christians, it is a religious matter. To Moslems it is a civil contract entered into by two families. This contract specifies the amount of dowry to be paid by the groom, some of which is held back in case of divorce, and the rest is spent by the bride's family for her clothing, linens, jewelry, and so on. Polygamy is regulated by the Koran, where it is written that a man with more than one wife should treat them equally, provide a house for them each, and care for them and their children. However, while not uncommon, polygamy is diminishing because supporting more than one family is a great burden economically. Today fewer than 8 per cent of Iraqi men have more than one wife. Because the law in the Koran was greatly misused, the government enacted "personal laws" under which a second marriage could be entered into only with the permission of a *qadi,* or judge; it is considered invalid if this permission is not obtained.

A man can divorce his wife at will, according to Moslem law, by merely saying three times in front of a witness, "I divorce thee." The wife has a similar right only if it is specifically stated in the marriage contract. This seldom happens, for the women of Iraq try to hold the family together. A divorced woman is at a great disadvantage, for it is difficult for her to remarry, and the blame for the divorce is usually laid to her. She and her children usually return to her family to live, but when the children reach the age of seven the father has the right to take them from her.

However, no real marriage problem exists in Iraq, and the single woman is rare. Practically all men take wives, for marriage, to a man, is proof of his manhood.

Marriage between different religious sects is not favored. A Moslem can marry outside his faith, but his wife must become a Moslem. However, a Moslem girl who marries a non-Moslem usually ends up murdered by her outraged family. But such a marriage is very rare.

Even in the cities and towns, though education, travel, communication, and a great increase in industrialization have weakened family ties to a certain extent, the ancient traditions of family obligation are adhered to quite strongly still.

In urban areas, among uneducated classes and strict conformers to custom, segregation of the sexes and rigid social mores are carried even farther than in the rural regions. For example, a man is permitted to talk only with the women of his immediate family before he marries. The veil is still the rule rather than the exception. The veil itself was put into use in Iraq during the days of the decline of

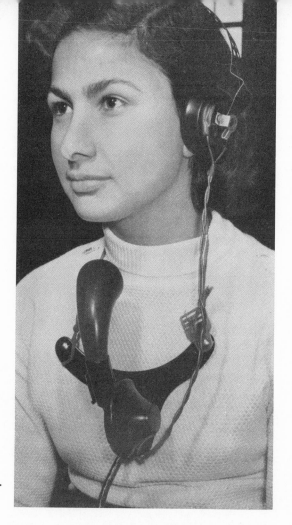

An Iraqi telephone operator in Baghdad.

the caliphate, as a protective measure for women of the upper classes. Actually, it was a practice developed much earlier, during the heyday of the Babylonian and Assyrian civilizations, to distinguish the free woman from the slave; the Moslems had adopted it from those they conquered.

Among the more educated classes today, however, it is not greatly in evidence. Though the discarding of the veil came about gradually and not through legislation, it has nevertheless proved a symbol of the emancipation of women, and has helped them to gain freedom in many areas. Women now have the right to vote. If she is of the more educated class, a woman may choose her own husband, live in her own household away from the titular head of the family, take part in demonstrations, and even deliver lectures in public. Teaching is the most common occupation for women wishing to work in Iraq, but there are women lawyers, judges, and diplomats.

Family life still remains bound up in ancient traditions. There is a curious blending of East and West when a household consists of two or more generations, each with a different outlook. Adherence to strict family traditions is required by the elders, but the young people are beginning to find it hard to go along.

City youth in Iraq are fascinated by Western ways, and a teen-age girl, unless she lives in some remote village or small town, is very

College students in a science class.

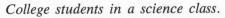

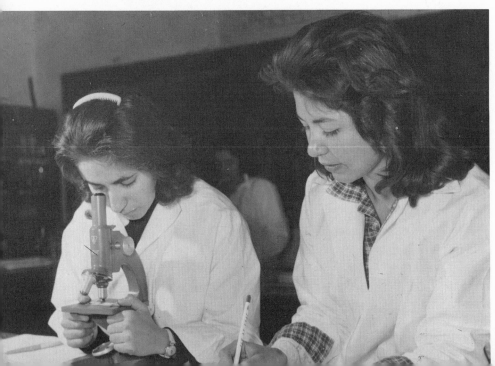

much like one of our own. She loves going to the movies, and has her favorite stars and singers. But unlike her Western counterpart, she will not date. In college, boys and girls are allowed to study together, but off the campus they separate. Even if a girl drives her own car, she must always be chaperoned when in the company of boys.

Among the working class in the towns and cities, men's social life is at home or in the coffeehouse. Those who are better off and more educated see each other in social or professional clubs. The women meet in each other's homes. It is the custom among well-to-do city women to hold a *qabul* or "at home" on a fixed day each week or so. In their Western-style homes these women entertain their friends, play cards, and generally behave very much as their sisters do the world over.

Before the 1958 revolution there did exist to a certain extent an elite class, made up for the most part of the royal family and its entourage and the high-up members of the government. But today social stratification, as such, has been abolished. Regardless of origin, women in Iraq meet in each other's homes with emphasis only on what each can contribute to the group as a whole.

The hospitality and generosity of the people of Iraq are a byword, and foreigners are quick to appreciate it. It is at the receptions, the dinners, and the social functions that this hospitality manifests itself, where the full resources of the country's cuisine are exhibited—rice cooked with almonds, kebab, eggplant with leban or yogurt, a whole roast lamb stuffed with rice, meat and spices.

✤ 13 ✤

Iraq Looks to the Future

IN THE MID-TWENTIETH CENTURY, the tide of nationalism that was gaining strength all over the world reached the borders of Iraq. Her people woke up and began to hope that the poverty, disease, ignorance, and ruin that were the result of centuries of foreign despotism and occupation could be wiped out. Thanks to mass communication and easier transportation they learned something of how the rest of the world lived, and they began to believe that their own people deserved and could get a better way of life. They determined to improve matters, and in this oldest habitat of man a new nation came into being.

Like many new nations, Iraq was confronted by clashing ideologies and by international economic intrigue over valuable natural resources such as oil. The line between "economic aid from abroad" and "foreign exploitation" is a thin one, especially for a new nation desperately in need of help. And in this period following the creation of an independent monarchy in the early 1920s the cry was "Pan-Arabism," and "Neutralism," and *"Wataniyya," "Qawmiyya,"* and "Iraq for the Iraqis."

In the more than four decades of independence real progress has been made, in the realm of education especially. Schooling is for everyone, regardless of religion, color, or place of birth, and it is

144

free. Today's physicians, lawyers, teachers, politicians, army officers, architects, and engineers were produced under this system. Many of them came from remote desert villages, from the marshlands of the south and the wind-swept highlands of the north. Today these distinguished products of an enlightened educational point of view are leading their country toward a better way of life.

Improvements are hard to bring about all at once, and progress is very slow. People are impatient, and because they are impatient there is conflict, political conflict. In Iraq this is not the same as it is in America or in Britain. Politics throughout the Middle East are sharper, more bitter, rougher and more drastic. Tempers are hotter and flare more swiftly. Political changes are drastic and usually come about through some sort of revolution. In this kind of political climate a new regime took over in Iraq in July 1958 under Abdel Karim Kassem. Kassem literally eliminated the monarchy and its supporters and established a republic. This government lasted only until February, 1963, when the Iraqi Army took over, and Kassem was killed. In November of the same year, in another military coup, Marshall Abdel Salam Aref seized power, swinging Iraq toward the Egyptian camp in the Middle East.

Any new nation is faced with a tremendous complex of problems, and Iraq is no exception, though its problems are made greater by the cold war between the West and the East that has existed since the end of World War II. The new government is socialist, but not communist, and is vitally concerned with the goal of Arab unity. It is neutral and resists commitments and alignments with any side except the Arab side. Its chief program is to solve the economic problems of the country.

Because Iraq is primarily an agricultural community, with about two thirds of its people dependent on the soil for their livelihood, the most important business before the new government is to make the country's agriculture more productive. Its long-range policy of rebuilding the economy on a modern basis has had three aims: land reform, flood control, and land reclamation.

The basic wealth of Iraq in terms of natural resources was still

there, although it had suffered from neglect and war. In addition to
the richness of sections of the land itself and the abundance of water,
there remained the enormous deposits of oil, minerals, and natural
gas. It is true that the climate in Iraq is suitable for the growing of
many products, but except for the north where the rainfall is sufficient, all depends on whether water is brought in enough quantity and
regularity to the crops. Of first importance in raising living standards, individual income, and the economic position of the country
as a whole was the increase of production by bringing water to the
thirsty soil. The most urgent need was to harness the annual flooding
of the great rivers that, uncontrolled, had washed out crops, houses,
and whole countrysides, and thus to utilize the country's natural water
supply.

A dam in the Dokan Gorge will reclaim 1½ million acres of land.

This landless farmer has just been presented by the Government with the deeds to a 60-acre irrigated plot of land which he himself can cultivate and on which he and his family will settle.

Today Iraq is no longer afraid of its periodic floods. Dams and other irrigation works control them, and are also used for land reclamation and electrification. The government is putting into effect an ambitious program covering new dams, regulators, bridges, siphons, culverts, water distribution by gravity and lift, silt clearance, installation of pumps on canals and rivers. The plans include the installation of plants which will in time supply water and electricity to the country's 9,000-odd villages and the two million people who live in them.

One of the first laws passed in the summer of 1958 when the Kassem regime came to power was the Agrarian Reform Law. The land that it is possible to cultivate in Iraq exceeds 48 million acres in area, but only about 23 million acres are actually under cultivation. The reform law limited ownership of land to 600 acres of irrigated land and 1,200 acres of land dependent on rainfall. All land over the limit was requisitioned by the government for distribution among landless farmers, in return for compensation in the form of bonds. The resulting reclamation and cultivation of a great area of land has already made possible considerable increase in productivity, and the agricultural economy is at last on a modern footing. The government has established farmers' cooperatives, maintained model farms, set up a veterinary department for control of animal disease, and worked out ways of educating farmers to modern ways and machines. And it has continued the already existing agricultural bank to help farmers with loans.

While barley and wheat form the largest bulk products, with about a million metric tons produced each year, it is their dates for which Iraqi growers are known all over the world. From the country's 30 million date palms come over 480,000 tons of dates, about 80 per cent of the world's supply. There are two harvesting seasons in Iraq: wheat, barley, and oilseeds, sown in autumn and watered by winter rains, are harvested in early summer, while rice, tobacco, sesame, maize, and millet are sown in the spring months and harvested in late summer.

It was not really until after World War II that the people of Iraq were able to get any sense of what modern industrialization meant, what it was like, how it could improve their own living standards. The shops and little craft factories of the bazaar, usually owned by a single family and passed down from generation to generation, supplied the simple needs of the people in cities, towns and outlying or rural areas. During the British mandate of Iraq a more modern point of view could be found among those well enough off to use goods from other sections of the country or even from other parts of the world. But the administration believed that full industrialization was impractical, and the people had to wait still longer for the many conveniences of modern life as we know it.

Today, however, the present government is eager to encourage the setting up of factories and plants so that many goods and services formerly imported from abroad can be handled within the country. A Ministry of Industry has been set up to supervise the establishing of industries and to encourage private investment as well as public. The Industrial Bank, founded in 1955, is now under the control of the ministry, and it grants loans, gives guidance and technical direction. As in many other young countries, or those involved in the change-over from a predominantly agricultural economy to one that at least encompasses industry, the government allows certain tax exemptions and other favorable measures to permit its citizens to operate industries that will benefit the country as a whole. Oil refining, and electrification, cement, cotton and wool spinning and weaving, are the most important government-operated industries, while those in which private capital is invested include cement, tanning, vegetable oils and soap, cotton and wool spinning and weaving, the tourist trade, transport, jute, and cigarettes. Out of a labor force of roughly three million, industry employs 100,000 and commerce 150,000.

A modern cotton factory in Baghdad.

Although Iraq today must still be considered among the under-developed countries of the world, there is real hope and expectation that this will not always be the case. There is plenty of living-space and so far no problem of overpopulation. But the chief reason for optimism lies in the sea of oil that lies beneath the surface of the earth. Iraq stands sixth in the world in volume of oil produced, barreling out over 40 million tons per year. Under the agreement which grants the government 50 per cent of oil profits, this means that the revenue share falling to Iraq in an average year is over $266 million. When we look at the national budget figure of about $320 million, we readily see that it is its oil that gives the country its financial equilibrium.

Although education in early Islam was voluntary, in the centuries that followed, Moslem men and theologians used education as a basis for religious instruction. They believed that children should not only be taught how to pray but also how to read, for how else would they be able to know the Koran, whose teachings were at the core of the Moslem way of life? They even advocated obligatory education for all, rich and poor alike. But most people could not, in fact, read or write. Even today, with schooling actually compulsory, il-literacy is still widespread; its eradication is one of the primary aims of the government of Iraq. Real progress, the administration believes, is not possible when a large number of the people cannot read or write.

While traveling around the countryside, through the central or southern hot and dusty desert villages, or in the cool, grassy uplands of the north, it is not at all unusual to come across seven or eight children sitting on the ground. They wear the flowing white *dish-dasha,* or robe, and small skullcap pushed back on their heads, and many of them have walked for miles from farm or neighboring vil-lage to attend these classes. They sit grouped around their mullah.

Schools and school children in the towns and cities of Iraq look more familiar. There are school buildings, laboratories, playgrounds, and nurseries. These and the young children playing outside of them are much like our own. There is one difference, however: all the students are in uniform, a different color for each grade. One can tell at a glance just where each one stands academically. The children who cannot afford them are given these uniforms free, and also hot lunches in the middle of the day. For others the cost is small. As in many of our cities, children go half fare in buses and streetcars. But they and their teachers also pay only half fare throughout the country on any sort of public transportation. There are Boy Scout and Girl Scout troops active in the cities, and one might even catch sight of a game of baseball being played after school hours—it is becoming very popular among the Iraqi.

Schooling is now free in all its stages, open on an equal footing to all citizens of the country, regardless of race, language, religion, nationality, sex or social status. The young government feels that any gains in raising the standard of the population as a whole and any important changes in the structure of the society must ultimately depend on education. Roughly 17 per cent, or the equivalent of $53.2 million, of the national budget was allocated to education for the year 1960–61, and this does not include a grant to the University of Baghdad or $120 million allocated to education over the next several years by the Planning Board. Since the summer of 1958, 400 new primary schools have opened, and there are now 3,000 throughout the entire country, serving nearly 700,000 students. There are about 120,000 students attending the 370 secondary schools, and about 40,000 girls and boys who go to the 72 private primary and secondary schools in Iraq. There was a great surge in enrollment in all schools, an increase of 57 per cent after the revolution of 1958. There were 46 per cent more teachers, 40 per cent more schools. Although the government has changed hands again since then, the trend toward more education has continued.

In Iraq a child spends six years in elementary school, and then must pass a national examination before he is permitted to continue into secondary school, which is made up of a three-year intermediate course and two years of college-preparatory work. This totals eleven, instead of the twelve-year program as carried out in the American system.

At the top of the educational pyramid is the University of Baghdad, made up of sixteen colleges and schools. Its enrollment is more than 12,000, and almost three thousand of these are women. The university campus, located in the city's southern suburbs, is nearly completed. Its cornerstone was laid in 1957; its architect was the world-famed Walter Gropius. It is hoped by the Iraqi that their university will be one of the foremost institutions of higher learning in the Middle East.

The government realizes that there is a vast need for new teachers, and in order to make the profession inviting it offers certain inducements: for example, teachers have hospitalization and medical care completely free, without time limit; and the children of teachers receive priority in college admission.

Of course there are young people who are not inclined toward an academic career, and in Iraq they are encouraged to train themselves in the technical and industrial fields so that the country's level of industrial technology will continue to rise. There are many technical

Men working on a drilling rig.

and vocational training schools, which graduate thousands every year. The Ministry of Education is continuing the Fundamental Education Program through which young men and women are trained in specialized fields and then sent in teams to different centers in more remote, outlying areas to teach people hygiene, mental health, personal cleanliness, and handicrafts. Agricultural specialists help the farmers adopt more productive modern methods; they start 4-H clubs and promote an interchange of ideas among farmers and villages in various parts of the country. This program is also concerned with adult illiteracy, for 87 per cent of the people cannot read or write. A five-year plan has been started, with the help of UNESCO, and a special day in February 1960 was designated as Literacy Day. The plan, its motto "Each One Teach One," proved to be very successful in the provinces. UNESCO has also cooperated with the government in setting up a technical institute to train skilled technicians who can later become teachers themselves. Gifted young people are sent abroad by the government to specialize in academic or technical work, and in 1960–61 there were over 5,000 such students taking part in the overseas program.

Believing that the unsatisfactory health conditions of the country were in urgent need of improvement, the government has allocated funds for the building of more facilities and for the teaching of the simple rules of communal and personal hygiene. A government ministry operates and supervises most of the country's hospitals, clinics, and dispensaries, and the majority of the doctors in Iraq are officials of this department. The rural population needs this service the most, for among them disease, undernourishment, poverty, and ignorance are rampant. Yet the country depends on this segment of the people for its economic future.

It is a huge task, for health conditions in Iraq are poor. Her people have suffered from various diseases because of poor sanitation and contaminated water. The infant mortality rate is high. Malaria is the number-one killer in the countryside, while in the poorer sections of the cities intestinal diseases are common. Sandstorms and hot weather cause many varieties of eye diseases.

The new government that took over in 1958 and the newer regime that followed it in 1963 have made great efforts to improve health and welfare. But there are many obstacles to progress. Most people in the rural and desert regions still may live and die without ever having seen a doctor. There is but one doctor for every 3,500 citizens, and of course most of these are in Baghdad. Also superstition is very influential in the life of the people, many of whom believe in the evil eye and visit the Arabian equivalent of a witch doctor. After centuries of ignorance and subjugation, these people think that misfortune, sickness, poverty, and death are the acts of Allah: there is nothing anyone can do about it. It is fate, or Kismet.

The Ministry of Health is building more hospitals, clinics, and dispensaries throughout Iraq. In 1961 there were only a hundred general hospitals—but this was a dramatic improvement over the past, for in 1918 there was but one. Medical schools in Baghdad and Mosul are being helped to expand facilities so that a larger number of students, health personnel, nurses, and social workers can be trained there. It is planned to expand the anti-malaria campaign so that the disease will be wiped out within a few years; as part of this plan, drinking water is gradually being piped to all the country's villages.

Up until a year or so ago cities and towns in Iraq grew at random, sprawling out haphazardly in all directions. But today the government is faced with a problem that always seems to go with a society becoming more and more industrialized, and this is the housing shortage. New low-income housing projects are going up in the cities, and wide streets, well lighted and paved, are being cut through ancient winding alleyways, with trees and shrubs being planted alongside. While outside the cities one still sees mostly the familiar clusters of mud huts, 30,000 new dwelling units have been started, and the crowded population can look forward to far more pleasant and comfortable homes.

There are roughly three million workers in Iraq's labor force. Half of these are in agriculture. In the past, laws governing employment conditions were weak and not inclusive of all workers, farm labor in particular being left out. Today, however, labor laws and social security have been expanded to cover most of the country's workers. These laws regulate working conditions, minimum wage, compensation for accidents and disabilities, old-age benefits, maternity and sick leave, unemployment, and holidays.

Widows, orphans, the disabled, and dependents of prisoners all have some coverage under the law. During 1959, nearly $800,000 was paid in social security benefits.

There is not much doubt that Iraq today plays a role in world affairs, because of its strategic location and its oil fields. Any quickening of the political pulse in Baghdad is sure to be felt immediately in other Middle East capitals. The whole region is in constant ferment, and the uneven development of the countries, some of them

A new housing area in Sulaimaniya.

still attached to ancient ways and others determined to be modern nations, keeps this ferment constantly simmering, if not boiling. Sometimes the newspapers of the world give prominence to sensational stories of *coups d'état* in Iraq, or revolts, uprisings against the government in power by some abused or neglected element or minority. But one must bear in mind when reading these stories that Iraq is a new nation politically. It is a country beset with countless internal problems caused by the heterogeneous nature of its population, a population containing many varied minority groups separated from each other by age-old barriers of religion, language, customs, geographic and climatic influences. Only time and astute leadership can solve these problems. The country's leaders today must feel their way through many trials and many errors.

Iraq stands today on the threshold of a new historical era. As a new nation it needs understanding, patience, and help. Iraqis are generally intelligent and quick to learn if given the opportunity. Today thousands who never before had the chance are using their free time in learning to read, in building strong bodies, in planning a good future for their children and grandchildren in this new nation in an old land. Among her young people of today are the leaders of what it is hoped will be a bright tomorrow. It is they who will lead their country to join the others in building a better world in which to live. *Wa Alla A'alam*—only God knows the future.

Index